Never Mind the Burdocks
A YEAR OF FORAGING IN THE BRITISH ISLES
SPRING EDITION / MARCH - MAY
VOLUME I
by Emma Gunn
Self published by Emma Gunn in Cornwall,
Summer 2014. First Print.
Printed and bound in the South West, UK.
Copyright Emma Gunn 2014
Designed and print managed by
Leap – design for change
www.leap.uk.net
ISBN 978-0-9929693-0-1

 Nevermind The Burdocks

 @Nmtheburdocks

The contents of this book have been researched and checked for accuracy, no infringement of any third party rights has been intended. Any errors or amendments that remain will be corrected in subsequent editions.

Due to climatic and environmental changes, species are affected so for example plants may emerge earlier or later than mentioned in the book. I have endeavoured to be as accurate as possible.

It is advisable for those with known allergies or those who may be potentially vulnerable such as pregnant or nursing mothers, the young, the elderly and invalids to be aware and decide whether or not to try edibles and recipes in this book.

FOREWORD

written by Sir Tim Smit KBE, founding director, the Eden Project

When we began the Eden Project, despite its grand architectural ambitions, we were seeking to do something unbelievably simple – to build a place which could teach us humility at the richness and variety of the bounty of the natural world. We are totally dependent on it and yet, culturally, many of us have been sleepwalking into a mind-set that saw nature as something apart from ourselves. Once such a view takes hold on a grand scale we will take it for granted and that way damnation lies for we will not steward or respect the world in a sustainable way and not many years down the line billions of people will pay for this arrogance.

Some years ago, when restoring the Lost Gardens of Heligan, with my friend, the late John Nelson, we worked with Peter Thoday (the advisor to the BBC's The Victorian Kitchen Garden"). He would always remind us that as late as the middle of the nineteenth century 75% of the population of Britain depended on foraging in the hedgerows for at least some of their food and almost all their medicinal plants. This is unbelievably recent and at first sight seemed implausible, yet, on reading Emma Gunn's marvellous little books on foraging you start to see the world through different eyes. You might say "there's none so blind as those that will not see", but as your eyes adjust to the humble hedgerows and you start to recognise the staples and delicacies available in the wild, you feel a strange calm. In these little books resides a roadmap to both survival and pleasure and perhaps a gently spiritual message, that we can all depend on the wild were we to learn again what to look for. Some might say this is an affectation, a luxury fad followed by people with a penchant for the "alternative" lifestyle. I would say different. I would say that here, in every hedgerow in the land lie the parents of the staples we have become familiar with. They grow quietly without the froth of special breeding, but have in them, nonetheless the vigour that makes them survivors and, more than that, a resilient bank of variety that lies untampered with by humankind.

So… I heartily recommend these books because, with every use your delight and wonder at the natural world grows and while your palate may take a while to familiarise itself with some of the flavours on offer, you will feel a strange and profound satisfaction at being so connected to the land and able to see what is on offer there as if once blind you have had your sight restored. This is an unadulterated delight. Don't just read these books – go forage - and be happy!

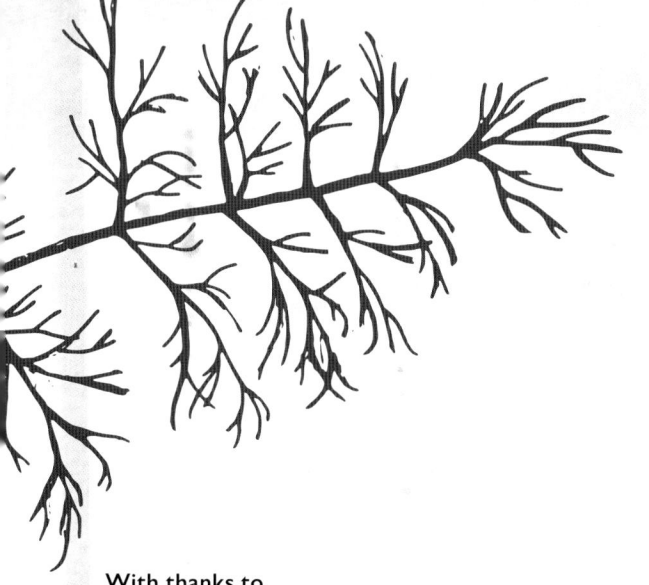

With thanks to…

Mum, Dad, Nik, Matt Hocking, Nathan Fletcher and Jessy Edgar from Leap (plus some of their interns), Bramble for accompanying me on walks, Jo 'Fancy Pants' Thomas, Tiana, Gill 'Hand' C, Pat Hudson, Sally and Andrew Snapes, Tim Ball, Robin Fuller, Steve Burrell for his brewing tips, Orlagh Murphy for her stunning artwork, Richard Buck with Fish and Forage, Luke Fox, Tim Pettitt my fungus guru, all my food-guinea pigs for testing out my food, Nathalie Frankson from Follow me fitness, Tim Smit for the foreword, James Strawbridge, Hamilton twins, all those who have encouraged me…

Dedicated to Matt, Esme and Grace Hocking.

Designed and produced as responsibly as possible by Leap - design for change. An ISO14001 independent design studio based in Cornwall, creating branding, design for print and website's for projects all over the world. Their studio is powered by Good Energy, they only use recycled or sustainable materials where possible in their triple bottom lined creative work. www.leap.uk.net

This book has been printed on 130gm2 silk (FSC Mix 70%) for the text pages and 350gm2 silk (FSC Mix 70%) for the cover. Using vegetable based inks and has a Carbon Neutral footprint.

CONTENTS

HOW TO USE THIS BOOK

On each day there is an edible item, be it a plant, mushroom, fish or other, starting with its scientific name. This is crucially important as this can truly identify the plant, fish or otherwise. The reason it is so important is that there are many common names for one plant for example but only ever one scientific name which is universally used. If using a plant for food or medicine you can imagine how important it is that you have the right plant because this could be the difference between life and death!

Next is the common name, this will aid you in recognising the plant, fish, shellfish, seaweed or mushroom. This may not be what you call it but this is a great example of why the scientific name is needed.

A synonym is an 'old' scientific name used for the plant which may be what you know the plant as but has been updated due to perhaps its physiology, chemical make-up or otherwise.

The name origin is where its scientific name or common name comes from. I love this part as it can tell you a lot about where something is from, who discovered it, its colour, texture, growth patterns for example annual, biennial, perennial, in what season you would find it, the shape of it, where you would find it... the list is endless. This isn't just Latin but it can be a melange of many languages including Greek, Sanskrit, Old English, Germanic, etc.

The family of a plant is a group that pulls together characteristics that link many plants. For example the Brassicaceae family, otherwise known as the mustard family is simply a group of plants that all produce flowers with 4 petals in a cross shape and contain sulphur compounds. Sometimes, just knowing this can help with understanding the plant and how you can recognise it or how you can eat it.

Where it's found and edible part are self-explanatory. Where it's found is absolutely crucial for fungus forays as mushrooms are extremely specific so if you know a certain species likes growing only under beech trees, then you will not have discovered it under perhaps an oak. Edible part can be just as important as there are certain plants where it is safe to eat the young shoots but the fruits are seriously poisonous.

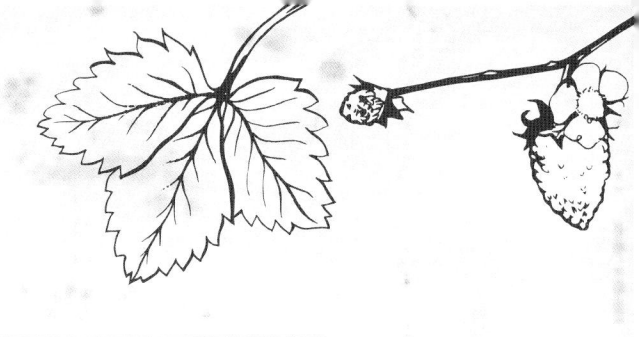

Edibility rating spans from 1-5, 1 being edible but pretty poor tasting and 5 is for the most tasty foraged food. This is my rating so you may disagree with the number I have given at times but everyone's taste buds are different so feel free to change the number to suit yourself.

Cautions are a guide as to what possible issues people may have with this item, for example if you are on any medication, pregnant or suffer from any health issues, then this will guide you as to whether this plant is safe for you to eat or not. This is something you need to do with food in general as people have allergies, some need to avoid certain foods for health issues, etc.

Where I have food ideas, this is again to guide you as to which bits you can eat, a guide as to how to prepare them and hopefully something you can take and run with. This can work with the recipe if there is one - try the recipe and if you like it, you may feel more confident eating the foraged food and trying it in your own recipes or day to day food. As I have learnt, do it gradually. I have tried a fully foraged meal before and been really disappointed! Try a little at a time or try to cook the item simply to see if your taste palate likes it.

Other info is to show that there are more to plants than meets the eye and to show they play and have played an important role in the life of humans for many centuries. This can be anything from medicinal uses to building materials.

Finally the last two titles are lookalikes and month span. For lookalikes this is to guide you away from possible similar plants that do more harm than good - have you seen 'Into the Wild'? Some plants, mushrooms, etc can look so similar but with one small difference can mean the difference between being very sick to having a tasty meal. Month span is to show you how long the foraged item is available for. This can be to help you eat it at its best or if it is shellfish, then to help you avoid them when it is their breeding season or when they are most likely to pick up bacteria in the warmer months that may cause you stomach upsets. (With plants, roots are best in autumn and winter as this is when they are storing their starches and sugars so during this period, the flowers, leaves or shoots tend to taste quite bitter as the plant is putting its energy into seeing it through the winter).

TIPS ON FORAGING

Any wild food must be treated as any new food which may cause allergies in certain people and not others - try out a little first and if no allergic reaction after a good length of time, then try more.

MUSHROOMS:

- There is no difference between mushrooms and toadstools, except people tend to call edible fungi 'mushrooms' and poisonous or toxic ones 'toadstools'.
- When picking fungi, ideally use a knife to harvest so you leave the mycelium (roots) behind so it can keep producing more fungi.
- Fungi species need to be kept separate from each other in case there is a toxic one in the batch. Fungi can contaminate other fungi.
- There are no rules of thumb that tell you whether a fungus is safe or not, so for example you can't tell if a fungus is safe or not by its gill colour.
- Only eat fungi when you are 100% sure what it is - consult a good guide, ask an expert, be certain and be safe.

Identify a fungus by looking at all of the below...
- Where it is growing - field, specific tree species, dead wood, etc.
- What time of year you find it
- Does it have a smell
- What colour is it
- Does it have a volva (egg shaped sac from which the stem grows)
- What do the gills look like
- Spore print
- Cap size
- Does it bruise when cut or pressed
- Does it have a ring on the stem

Once you have checked through all of these and it points at one specific edible fungus, then try it in small quantities as you may be allergic to it.

| ROOTS: | • You can only uproot plants if you have the landowner's permission and as long as it is not a rare or endangered species.
• If you dig up roots, then remember that plant will die. Only pick prolific plants. |

| FRUITS & BERRIES: | • Fruit colour does not identify whether it is safe or not. Raspberries, hawthorn fruits and rowan berries are all red, where edible black fruits include sloes, blackberries and black currants.
• Check the foliage of the plant before picking the fruit to help you identify the plant correctly.
• Be aware that certain toxic fruiting plants are climbers such as briony and honeysuckle and can entwine themselves in other plants so be careful what you are picking.
• Leave plenty for wild life to eat.
• Only harvest what you will eat. |

| LEAVES: | • Harvest edible leaves from a clean source and do not pick anything that is less than perfect. Imperfections can be caused by herbicide sprays, soil pollutants, insect damage, etc.
• If picking edible plants that live in or by water, check the water quality and water source. Plants such as watercress can contain liver fluke from sheep which can be destroyed by cooking.
• Leave most plants and especially shoots behind so the plant can photosynthesize - with very few leaves, the plant will struggle to grow.
• Remember there can be lookalikes of plants so use your senses - if the plant is meant to be fragrant, smell it. If rough, feel it. If shiny, have a look, etc. |

FLOWERS:	• Leave plenty of flowers on a plant for insects to feed on, for pollination but also for fruits to harvest later in the year. • Pick flowers when it is sunny to get the best flavour or fragrance from them, for example honeysuckle flowers for making syrup or wine. • Only pick what you need and will use. • Don't pick rare or endangered flowers.

SEAWEEDS:	• Pick seaweeds using scissors so the plant can regrow. • Sea creatures use seaweeds to hide and live in so take sparingly. • Only harvest perfect looking species. • Only harvest seaweeds that are attached to rocks rather than washed up on the shore. The seaweed may have been out at sea for ages before being washed up so the quality of it as a food is diminished.

TIDES:	• Respect the sea. Purchase a tide timetable for the area you will be foraging as the tides differ all around our coast. • Keep an eye on the tides - you don't want to be cut off by the incoming tide and always have an escape route. You may be trapped on land for example on rocks but with no way to get back to safety. • At low tides, weever fish bury themselves in the sand where unsuspecting people may stand on them and the fish injects venom into the person's foot. A way of avoiding this is to wear suitable footwear at low tides if paddling in shallow water. If you do get stung, put the affected area in as-hot-as-you-can-handle water without scalding yourself.

CLIFFS:	• Do not get too near the edge of a cliff. There is the potential to fall but also there may be very little ground beneath you, for example a cave. • When harvesting plants on or near a cliff, be aware that the cliff may not be stable and there is always potential for a landslip. • Do not attempt to climb up a cliff for wild food - the likelihood is you can find the same plant in a safer place. You do not want to cause unnecessary damage to the environment or yourself.

WEATHER:	• Dress suitably for the weather or take provisions with you if you are going to be out for a long time. • If you are going to be out for a while in the cold, wear a hat and gloves and keep warm. Wear suitable shoes - if wearing wellies, wear thick socks. • If it is warm and sunny, protect your head to limit the likelihood of getting sunstroke. Wear sun cream, take a long sleeved top with you and if you are out in the evening, the temperature can drop so take warm clothes with you. • As this is the UK, the weather can change for the worse quite quickly. Take wet weather gear with you just in case!

As a rule of thumb...
Young tender leaves and spring flowers are available in spring
Flowers and berries are available in summer
Autumn is good for the majority of fungi, fruits and nuts
Winter is when roots are at their best as the plant is storing sugars

This is not definitive but a very rough guide.

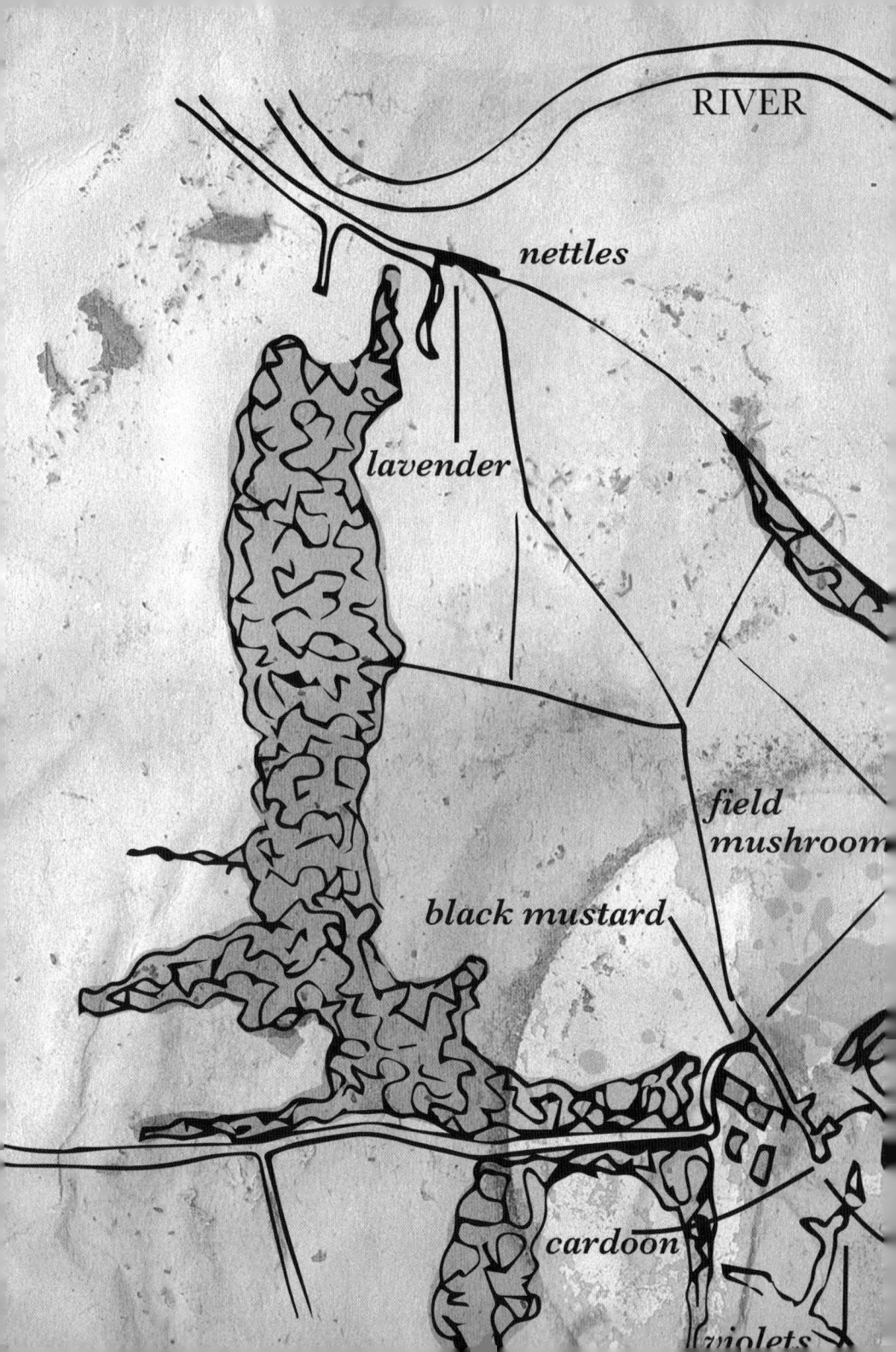

RIVER

nettles

lavender

field mushroom

black mustard

cardoon

violets

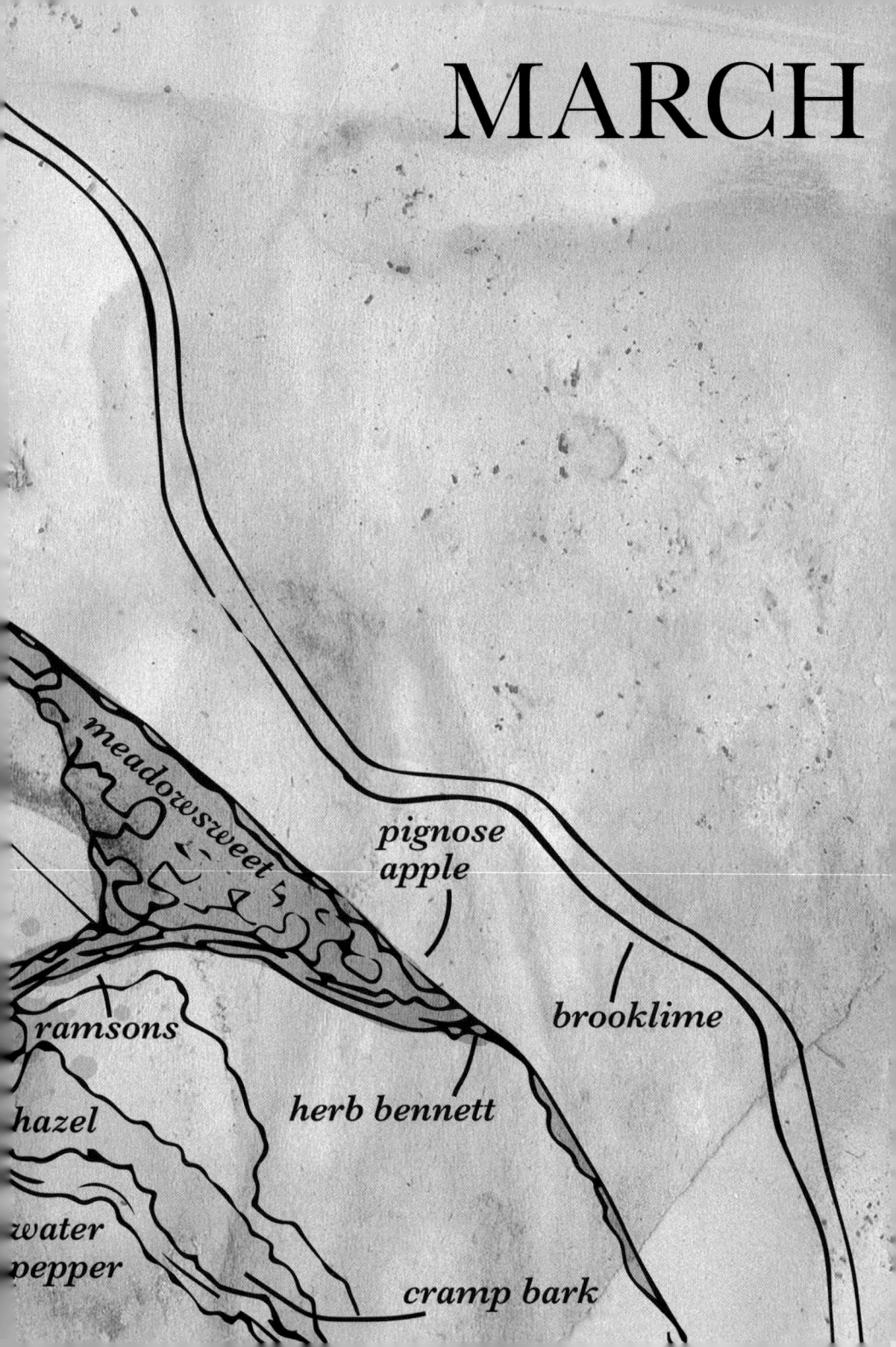

MARCH

meadowsweet

pignose
apple

brooklime

ramsons

herb bennett

hazel

water
pepper

cramp bark

DANDELION
Taraxacum officinalis

NAME ORIGIN:	*Taraxacum* comes from a Persian word meaning bitter pot herb. Dandelion is a corruption of the French dents-de-lion meaning lion's teeth, referring to the mane-like flowers and teeth-shaped leaves. In French, it's called piss-en-lit meaning wet the bed, due to its diuretic properties. *Officinalis* means of the apothecary's shop due to its medicinal properties.
FAMILY:	Asteraceae

EDIBLE PART:	Leaves, flowers (from March onwards) and roots (see Nov 2nd).
EDIBILITY RATING:	3
WHERE IT'S FOUND:	Lawns, meadows, waste ground.
CAUTIONS:	The latex (sap) from the leaves and stems can cause dermatitis on sensitive skin.
LOOKALIKES:	Other members of the Asteraceae family such as cat's ear (*Hypochaeris* sp.), hawkbit and hawksbeard (*Crepis* spp.) have similar flowers and leaves. All can be used in the same way as dandelions.
MONTH SPAN:	Leaves and roots available all year. Flowers available from March (Hz 5).

FOOD IDEAS:	Force the leaves: cover young plants with a pot to block out the light. This makes the leaves elongate in search of light and they lose their bitterness in the process. Use them as a salad with a light dressing and some toasted seeds or garlic croutons. When the flowers appear later in the year (from April onwards) they make a delicious marmalade, cordial and wine, or just sprinkle petals on salads or desserts. It is best to remove the slightly bitter green parts of the flower.
OTHER INFO:	Remember blowing dandelion seeds to see what time it is? Blow dandelion clock, blow! One o'clock, two o'clock, three o'clock, four…

DANDELION MARMALADE

4 oranges
8 tbsp dandelion petals
water
jam sugar

Pop a small plate in the fridge. In a saucepan, grate the zest of all 4 oranges, then squeeze all the juice and any pulp. Measure the amount of liquid and add an equal amount of jam sugar and a splash of water. Add half the dandelion petals and start to heat gently. Stir occasionally and keep an eye on it to prevent sticking. Simmer gently for 20 - 30 minutes. To see if it's reached its setting point, spoon a little onto the cold plate, wait 20 - 30 seconds and push it with your finger. If it's set it will wrinkle. Stir in the rest of the petals and pour into a sterilized jar. Label and refrigerate.

SEA ASTER
Aster tripolium

NAME ORIGIN:	*Aster* comes from the Greek for star, *tri* means three and *polium* comes from *polis* meaning citizens or great men, such as Hippocrates, Galen and Dioscorides.
FAMILY:	Asteraceae

EDIBLE PART:	Leaves and stem (best before it flowers later in the year).
EDIBILITY RATING:	4
WHERE IT'S FOUND:	Salt marshes, coastal areas, salt river inlets.
LOOKALIKES:	Other asters grow by the coast but narrow glossy fleshy leaves and pale lilac flowers help identify *Aster tripolium*.
MONTH SPAN:	(Hz 6) Flowers from July - October. Leaves available most of the year.

FOOD IDEAS:	Use fresh in salads to add texture and slight saltiness. Steam and serve as a vegetable, or use to stuff fish. Can also be added to stews, fish pies, etc. It has the tiniest hint of angelica and a slight metallic taste to it. I think the leaves gently steamed or simmered with a little water and butter taste like fresh mackerel! Simple and delicious!
OTHER INFO:	This makes a lovely addition to the more obvious coastal vegetables. My favourite estuary now has everything from sea beet, rock and marsh samphire, sea plantain, sea purslane, salt bush and sea aster - this place is hard to beat! And no, I'm not telling where…

LAMB'S LETTUCE
Valerianella locusta

SYNONYM:	*Valerianella olitoria*
NAME ORIGIN:	*Valerianella* is a diminutive of the genus *Valeriana*. *Valere* in Latin means to be healthy. The Roman physician Valerius supposedly first used valerian as a drug.
FAMILY:	Valerianaceae

EDIBLE PART:	All aerial parts.
EDIBILITY RATING:	3
WHERE IT'S FOUND:	Cultivated ground, dry soil.
LOOKALIKES:	*Epilobium montanum* or broad-leaved willowherb looks similar but has glossier, deeper green leaves - also edible but not as tasty.
MONTH SPAN:	Leaves likely to be out from March, and can be definitively identified by the flowers which are out April - June.

FOOD IDEAS:	Great filler for salads. Use all aerial parts; the leaves are less bitter when they're young, and the flowers are delicately sweet - I think they taste like rice paper. Lamb's lettuce makes a great salad by itself with a simple dressing or mixed with other salad leaves such as watercress, miner's lettuce or spinach.
OTHER INFO:	This is a very common weed - always good to find! It's sometimes called corn salad, which refers to it often growing in wheat fields, and the European term for any grain is corn, e.g. corn dollies (made mostly from wheat, *Triticum* sp., not from corn, *Zea mays*). Cool bit of folklore, this plant also goes by the common name rapunzel. In the fairy tale, a woman pregnant with a little girl has cravings for the plant called rapunzel, so her husband sneaks into an enchantress' garden and gets caught picking some. As a bargain, the enchantress claims the child when it is born and names her... Rapunzel!

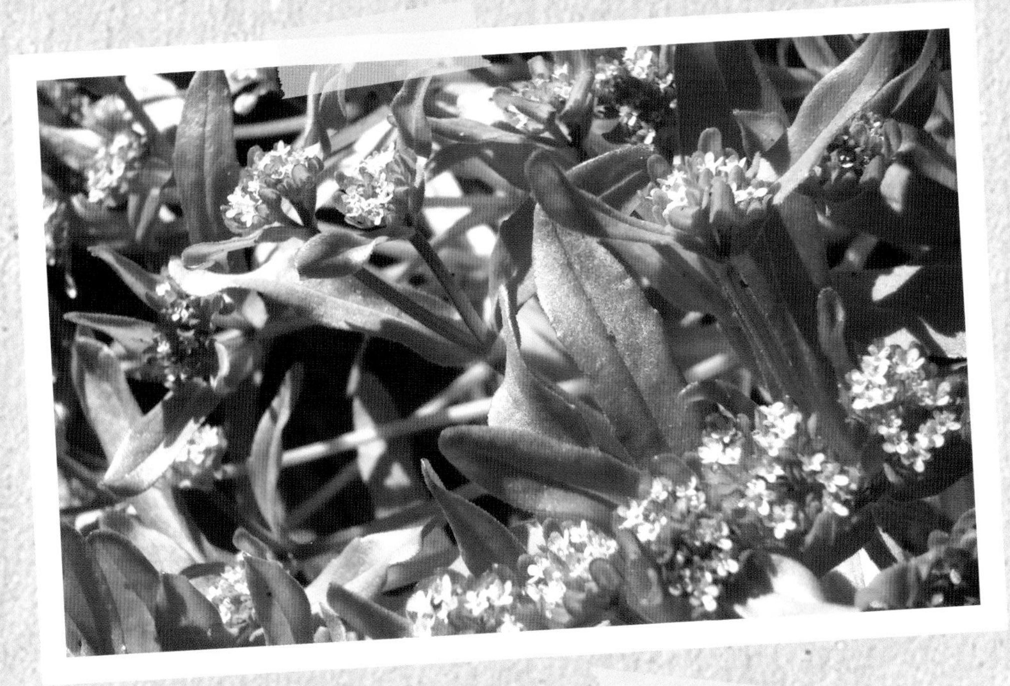

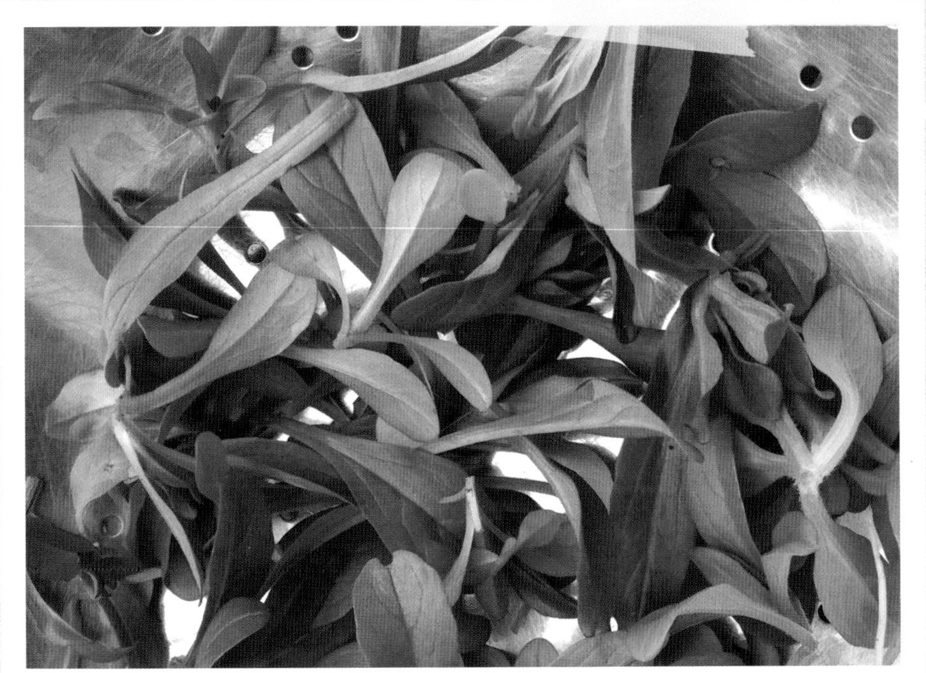

SINGAPORE CHILLI CRAB

(serves 2)

4 crabs
4 minced shallots
2 tbsp minced ginger
6 minced cloves of garlic
2 sticks of lemongrass
3 small hot chillies
1 tbsp peanut butter
2 tsp curry powder
splash of soy sauce
4 tbsp vegetable oil
1 tbsp brown sugar
2 tsp cornflour
1/2 cup water
1 tbsp tomato ketchup
1 cup coconut milk (optional)

One of my favourite dishes when we lived in Singapore. The first time I had it was when we were up near Changi where my friend Hannah lived. They had ceiling fans and no air conditioning, their local pool was filled with sea water and their decor was fishing paraphernalia - quite a refreshing change to the usual ice cold concrete apartment blocks. Down by the sea, we would have chilli crab with Orangina and Tiger Beer near the pier. Magical. There are many different variations of chilli crab but all have garlic, tomato paste and ginger. I prefer just using the claws and saving the bodies with the brown meat for a separate recipe like crab mousse.

In a food processor blitz shallots, ginger, garlic, lemongrass, chillies, peanut butter, curry powder and soy sauce. Pull off the crab claws and crack them. Heat the vegetable oil in a wok and cook the crab claws until they turn red. Add the spice mix and fry for a few minutes, turning the crab claws to coat them. Mix the cornflour, sugar and water together and add to the wok, stirring constantly. Add the ketchup and coconut milk if you are using it. Simmer for 5 minutes and serve. Use your fingers, it's a must!

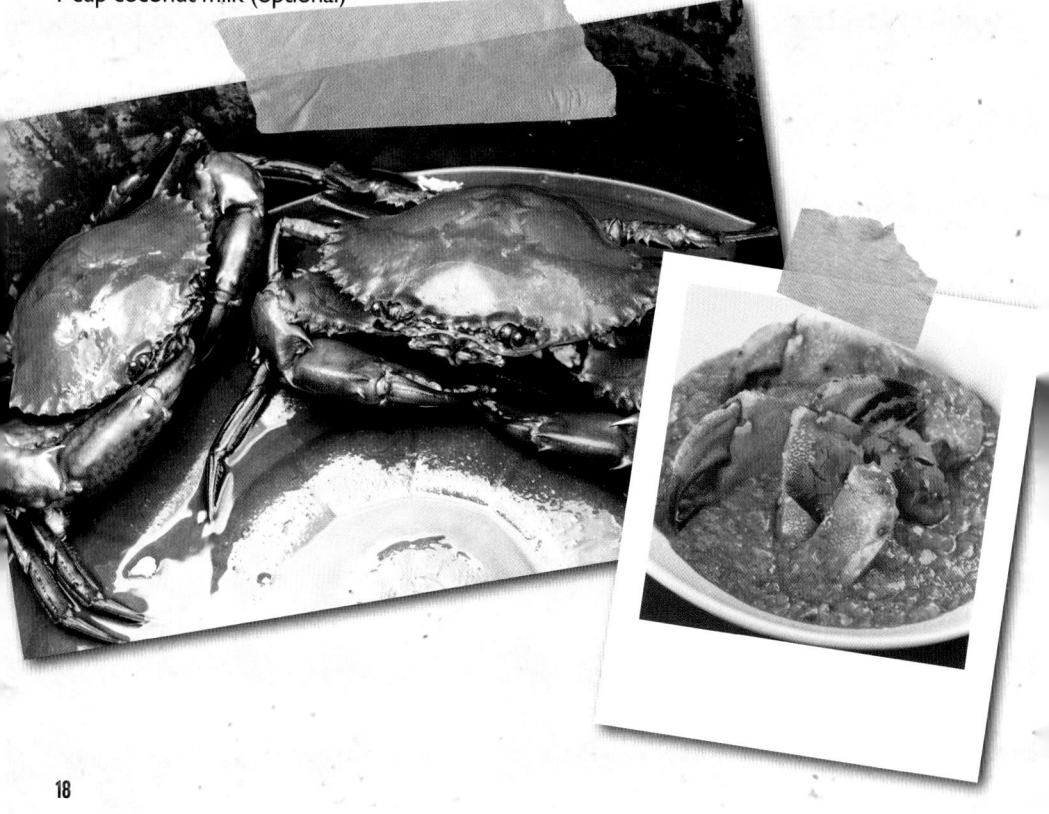

BROWN CRAB Edible crab
Cancer pagurus

NAME ORIGIN:	Cancer, meaning crab, like the star sign. *Pagurus* comes from the ancient Greek *pagouros*, which refers to edible crabs.
FAMILY:	**Cancridae**

EDIBLE PART:	Meat
EDIBILITY RATING:	4
WHERE IT'S FOUND:	Rock pools at low tide, in the sea.
CAUTIONS:	Avoid if you have shellfish allergies.
MONTH SPAN:	All year round, nearer coastline in summer.

FOOD IDEAS:	I think the best way is probably to boil up the crab whole, then pick out the meat and take your time making a meal of it!! Also good in sandwiches, soup, crab cakes and linguini. After boiling, leave it to cool - don't plunge it into cold water as it will soak up the water like a sponge and go soggy.
OTHER INFO:	The feathery gills are known as dead man's fingers - they're not poisonous as some people suggest, but they're tough and indigestible. Brown crab is also known as edible crab and must be at least 140mm across the carapace to be legally harvested, and don't take pregnant females. Try using crab pots or catch a very low spring tide and have a poke about rock pools that aren't normally exposed. Use a stick to poke around in holes but be careful as you don't want to damage the crab.

TO DRESS A CRAB, SEE PAGE 214

HERMIT CRABS
Pagurus bernhardus

NAME ORIGIN:	*Pagurus* comes from the ancient Greek *pagouros*, which refers to edible crabs.
FAMILY:	**Paguridae**
EDIBLE PART:	Use the whole animal for flavouring (or just the meat if you are a bit desperate for food!).
EDIBILITY RATING:	2
WHERE IT'S FOUND:	Sea, beaches.
CAUTIONS:	Avoid if you have shellfish allergies and collect from clean areas.
MONTH SPAN:	All year round.

FOOD IDEAS:	Probably only good for a crab bisque and other shellfish-based soups and sauces.
OTHER INFO:	You can pick these off bait pots or go to your nearest harbour and ask a fisherman if you could have any he catches. They are good for bait. Hermit crabs are funny little things. They have hard shell on their claws and a soft spiraling abdomen. As the crab grows, they have to slink out of the shell they're in and worm their little soft bodies into a larger shell as quickly as possible, like skinny dippers caught out without a towel! When I lived in Singapore, we would go to some stunning tropical islands off the mainland where I often saw hermit crabs. I tried to take one home as a pet but unfortunately it didn't work out too well…

HERMIT CRAB SOUP

For the stock:
6 cups of hermit crabs
1 peeled and sliced red onion
1 sliced celery stalk
1 chopped carrot
1/2 cup of dry white wine
10 peppercorns
a good pinch of sea salt
1 bay leaf
3 sprigs of thyme
1 small handful of parsley

Put the crabs in a large saucepan and cover with an inch of water. Simmer for an hour, skimming off any scum with a slotted spoon. When there is no more scum remove the hermit crabs and leave until cool enough to handle, then crack the shells with a rolling pin and return them to the stock water with the remaining ingredients and simmer for 20-30 minutes. Strain the lot and keep the liquid.

For the soup:
2 tbsp butter
1 large leek washed
3/4 cup of dry white wine
4 cups of hermit crab stock
2 tbsp tomato paste
1 1/4 cups double cream
a pinch of cayenne (optional)
sea salt to taste
fennel fronds to serve

In a large saucepan, melt the butter and fry the chopped leeks until tender. Add the wine, stock and tomato paste and simmer for 5 minutes. Blitz in a food processor or with a stick blender, return to the pan and add the cream. Heat through and season, adding the cayenne. Ladle into bowls and top with fennel fronds.

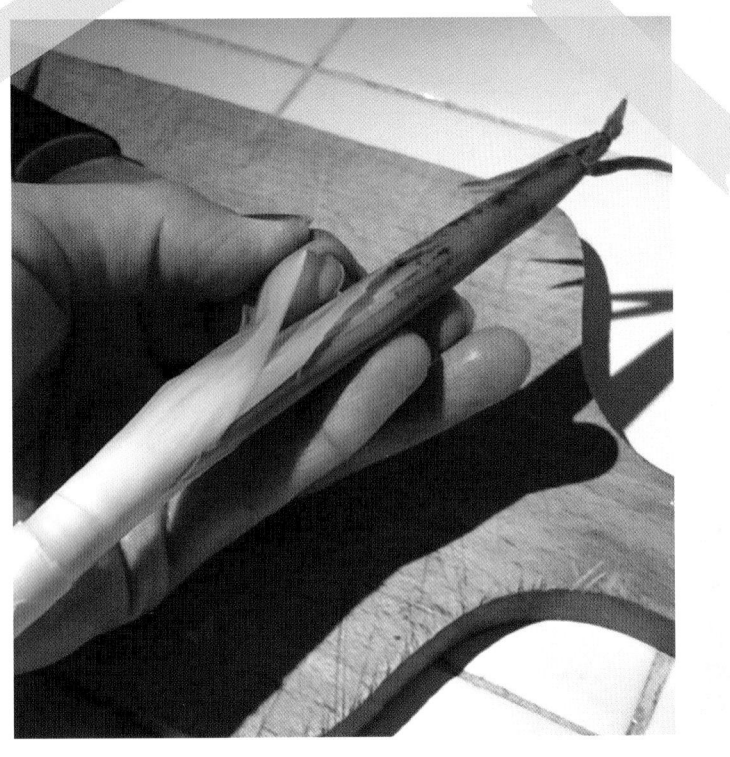

EDIBLE BAMBOO Moso

Phyllostachys edulis

SYNONYM:	*Bambusa edulis*
NAME ORIGIN:	*Phyllo* comes from the Greek for leaf, *stachys* means column and *edulis* means edible.
FAMILY:	**Poaceae**
EDIBLE PART:	Shoots
EDIBILITY RATING:	4
WHERE IT'S FOUND:	In gardens and elsewhere in moist dappled shade.
LOOKALIKES:	Bamboos all look pretty similar but through either good knowledge or trial and error, test out the different varieties to see if they're palatable.
MONTH SPAN:	Shoots appear from March (Hz 7).

FOOD IDEAS:	Eat the young shoots raw or cooked - when raw they can be a little bitter. Peel off any sheaths as they can have irritating hairs and are too fibrous to eat. Wash and finely slice. Use in stir fries, curries, dim sum, salads and Chinese-style broths.
OTHER INFO:	All bamboo shoots are edible, but there are quite a few that are bitter or a little irritating on the throat.

SEA LETTUCE
Ulva lactuca

NAME ORIGIN:	*Lactuca* means lettuce in Latin, and *lac* is Latin for milk referring to the white juice lettuce exudes. Sea lettuce is so called because of the broad green seaweed sheets that are vaguely reminiscent of broad lettuce leaves.
FAMILY:	**Ulvaceae**

EDIBLE PART:	Seaweed
EDIBILITY RATING:	4
WHERE IT'S FOUND:	Rock pools
CAUTIONS:	Unknown
LOOKALIKES:	Sea lettuce is related to gutweed but looks very different - sea lettuce looks like green translucent sheets.
MONTH SPAN:	All year round.

FOOD IDEAS:	Wrap whole fish in sea lettuce and pan fry or barbecue - it keeps the fish moist and adds a delicious crispy seaweed skin. Dry sea lettuce in the sun or in an oven on a low heat and use as a condiment - crumble and add it to soups, stews, stir fry, popcorn, etc. If you eat it raw, wash well to remove any tiny shells or sand. Use it to make the freshest sushi!
OTHER INFO:	Sea lettuce is extremely high in minerals and helps with healthy nails, hair and skin. It's high in both calcium and magnesium - magnesium helps the body absorb calcium, which helps prevent osteoporosis. It's also a valuable plant for dieting as it's high in dietary fibre but very low in calories, so will fill you up but won't fill you out! Did you know that chloroform is an organic compound that comes from various sources including acetone but naturally from many seaweeds, including sea lettuce?

EXPLODING
SEAWEED
BALLS

Washed fresh sheets
of sea lettuce
1/2 tub of cream cheese
1 long red chilli
1 large handful oregano
or marjoram
pinch of sea salt
black pepper
3 tbsp plain flour
1/2 tsp bicarbonate of soda
ice cold beer
or carbonated water
sunflower oil to deep fry

Finely chop the chilli and oregano and mix in a bowl with cream cheese and seasoning. Lay out the sheets of sea lettuce. Using a teaspoon, dollop a little ball of the cream cheese mix on each sheet, then roll up - you may need a couple of sheets of seaweed in a cross shape to completely cover the cream cheese. Start heating the sunflower oil ready for deep frying. In a separate bowl, mix the flour and bicarb. With a balloon whisk, slowly add the beer or carbonated water until well blended and the consistency of mustard (with no lumps!). Using a fork, gently coat the seaweed balls in the batter and gently add them to the hot oil (be careful as it could spit) and cook until golden. Fish out the crispy balls with a slotted spoon, put them on a plate with kitchen roll to drain away excess oil, and serve. Feel free to try out different fillings.

SELFHEAL
Prunella vulgaris

NAME ORIGIN:	*Prunella* in German is 'braume' meaning quinsy which it supposedly heals (quinsy is a complication of tonsillitis). *Vulgaris* means common.
FAMILY:	Lamiaceae
EDIBLE PART:	Raw or cooked leaves.
EDIBILITY RATING:	2
WHERE IT'S FOUND:	Grassland, waste ground, woodland edges.
LOOKALIKES:	The purple flowers of selfheal are quite striking but don't confuse the leaves with St John's wort *Hypericum perforatum*. A simple test is to hold up a leaf as St. John's wort leaves have tiny oil glands which contain the active ingredient for treating depression, whereas selfheal has no pin-prick oil glands in the leaves.
MONTH SPAN:	(Hz 3) Flowers July - September, seeds ripen August - September.

FOOD IDEAS:	Wash the leaves (this supposedly removes the tannins and makes it less bitter) and use them in salads and soups. A cold water infusion of the fresh or dried leaves makes a refreshing drink.
OTHER INFO:	Prunella is used medicinally as an anti-inflammatory, hence the name selfheal.

HOGWEED Cow parsnip

Heracleum sphondylium

NAME ORIGIN:	**Named after Hercules (who was also known as Heracles) who is said to have discovered its virtues.**
FAMILY:	**Apiaceae**
EDIBLE PART:	Young shoots, roots and seeds (which remain on the dried stalks through winter).
EDIBILITY RATING:	3
WHERE IT'S FOUND:	Woodland, grassland, hedgerow, ditches.
CAUTIONS:	The sap can cause serious blistering if you pick it in sunlight. I use scissors and gloves to harvest.
LOOKALIKES:	This is a fairly distinctive plant from the carrot family (Apiaceae).
MONTH SPAN:	(Hz 5) Flowers June - September, seeds ripen July - October but stay on the plant for use in winter.

FOOD IDEAS:	Strangely enough, hogweed is really delicious. The young shoots, washed and steamed make a good vegetable. They can be dipped in tempura batter and served with soy sauce and a little sesame oil. The seeds when dry and papery give an incredibly pungent orange peel/cardamom flavour, and make tasty shortbread or very unusual ice cream - one to get people guessing! The root can be dug up and eaten like parsnips (hence their common name cow parsnip).
OTHER INFO:	When you pick it, wear gloves, or gather it on a dull day, as the sap causes extreme photosensitivity and severe blistering, followed by scars that worsen when exposed to daylight. I had a great birthday a few years ago on 'John's Island' where we had a pirate treasure hunt, dressed as pirates and kayaked to the nearest pub and back in time to pitch our tents and camp. Somewhere along the way, I must have brushed past some hogweed, as the next day I woke up with a sore, blistered knee. Each time I exposed it to sunlight, it would darken and become irritated. It took a year for the scarring to go - be warned! If you go strimming, avoid this as it is juicy and will spray everywhere.

HOGWEED SEED ICE CREAM

1 to 2 umbels (seed heads)
of dried hogweed seeds
300ml double cream
300 ml milk
1 egg yolk
3 tbsp caster sugar

Pull the seeds off the seed head stalks and chop in half to release the seeds' flavour. Put in a saucepan with the cream and milk and heat - once reached a simmer, take off the heat and leave to infuse and cool for an hour. In a bowl beat the egg yolk and sugar together with a balloon whisk. Sieve out the seeds from the milk cream mix (keeping the liquid and discarding the seeds). Reheat the liquid, pour over the yolk sugar mix and return all of it to the saucepan, heating gently and stirring constantly with a wooden spoon. When the liquid has thickened and coats the back of the spoon, remove from the heat immediately and leave to cool. Either pour it into an ice cream maker to freeze or put it in a freeze-proof container with a lid. Pop it in the freezer for 1 hour, take out and stir to break up ice crystals and return to freezer. Repeat again after an hour and again once more. This is a delicious ice cream, which tastes quite buttery with a hint of the orange like flavour.

MINER'S LETTUCE
Claytonia perfoliata

NAME ORIGIN:	*Claytonia* is named after John Clayton, an American plant collector. *Per* means through and *foliata* means the leaf as the stem appears to pass through the leaf.
FAMILY:	**Portulacaceae**
EDIBLE PART:	Aerial parts
EDIBILITY RATING:	4
WHERE IT'S FOUND:	Moist light soil, semi shade.
LOOKALIKES:	*Euphorbia* sp. look similar to miner's lettuce and can be quite poisonous but euphorbias always exude a milky sap.
MONTH SPAN:	In leaf from late winter, flowers May - July.

FOOD IDEAS:	A beautiful shade of green, these dimpled shields are an excellent addition to a salad, if not just for their unusual shape, but also as they are refreshing and succulent. Miner's lettuce leaves can hold their own so you could have a miner's lettuce salad, dressing it with a light vinaigrette with ingredients such as lemon, garlic and perhaps a little dijon mustard. Once picked, wash the leaves well and serve pretty quickly - the leaves are quite succulent, so they can be easily bruised.
OTHER INFO:	I had seen this odd looking plant only in books until I stumbled across it at the back of plant sales at Eden (I always react to finding new plants as if I've struck gold).

JAPANESE QUINCE
Flowering quince

Chaenomeles speciosa

SYNONYM:	*Cydonia laganaria, Cydonia lagenaria, Cydonia speciosa, Pyrus japonica*
NAME ORIGIN:	The synonym *Cydonia* means quince in Greek. Cydonia was an ancient city in Crete, founded by King Cydon, where the modern-day Greek city Chania now lies. Common quince grew in abundance here.
FAMILY:	**Rosaceae**
EDIBLE PART:	Flowers and fruit (Fruit ripens in October). (For true Quince *Cydonia oblonga* see November 25th as the fruit is eaten and prepared in the same way).
EDIBILITY RATING:	3
WHERE IT'S FOUND:	Dappled shade, woodland, hedge, trained up a wall.
LOOKALIKES:	I may have confused you slightly but true or common quince is *Cydonia oblonga* where Japanese or flowering quince is *Chaenomeles speciosa*, but as I have mentioned they are both prepared in the same manner. Japanese or flowering quince used to share the same genus (see synonym) and is still in the same family.
MONTH SPAN:	Flowers February - June, fruits ripen October.
FOOD IDEAS:	Eat the flowers. The cooked fruit are good for making jam or jelly.
OTHER INFO:	When making jelly from the fruit, don't squeeze the juice through muslin, just allow it to drip so it comes out clear. The plant is often used as a decorative shrub or bush trained up a sunny wall.

" COME RIDE WITH ME THROUGH THE VEINS OF HISTORY... "

Enjoy listening to Muse?
These are the beginning lyrics for their song
Knights of Cydonia

BOG MYRTLE
Myrica gale

SYNONYM:	*Myrica palustris, Gale palustris*
NAME ORIGIN:	*Myrike* is the Greek name for a riverside shrub, *gale* is the old English name for bog myrtle and the Anglo-Saxon name for it was *gagel*.
FAMILY:	**Myricaceae**
EDIBLE PART:	Flowers and leaves.
EDIBILITY RATING:	2
WHERE IT'S FOUND:	Bogs, damp moorland.
CAUTIONS:	Abortifacient so avoid if pregnant.
MONTH SPAN:	(Hz 1) Flowers March - May, seeds ripen August - September.

FOOD IDEAS:	Use fresh or dried fruits and leaves for flavouring food, ales, schnapps and as a tea. It was believed to increase foaming in ale and beer, and it was mainly used as a flavouring until hops were favoured over this plant.
OTHER INFO:	A useful insect repellent, either make an infusion for your skin or hang a bunch of the leaves where you don't want insects - good for camping in Scotland!

WATTLE Acacia
Acacia dealbata

SYNONYM:	*Acacia decurrens* var. *dealbata*
NAME ORIGIN:	*Acacia* comes from the Greek word *akazo* meaning to sharpen (Egyptian thorn is called *Acacia arabica* from which gum arabic is obtained). The species *dealbata* means whitened referring to the leaves' light colouration.
FAMILY:	Fabaceae
EDIBLE PART:	Flowers, gum.
EDIBILITY RATING:	2
WHERE IT'S FOUND:	Gardens in full sun or dappled shade.
MONTH SPAN:	Flowers January - March (Hz 8).

FOOD IDEAS:	Eat the flowers cooked as fritters, as a flavouring or made into cordial. The gum that exudes from the plant can be chewed. Acacia honey is delicious and floral.
OTHER INFO:	I studied garden design at Pershore College in Worcestershire, one of the last pure horticultural colleges at the time. Outside my bedroom window was the most beautiful acacia and when I left the window open, I'd come back from lessons to find beautiful golden blossoms all over my room. This elegant plant grows naturally in warm temperate climates such as the Mediterranean and parts of Australia. The wood can be used for wood turning and the flowers and stems as cut flowers.

BIRCH SAP SYRUP

Try and collect as much birch sap as you can because when you make the syrup, the volume reduces dramatically! Pass your birch sap through a fine sieve or muslin cloth to remove any debris into a large saucepan and begin to gently simmer on a very low heat. The water in the liquid will evaporate and when the liquid turns a golden brown, it is ready. Be careful not to let the liquid burn. Serve with pancakes or a suitable dessert.

BIRCH

Betula pendula

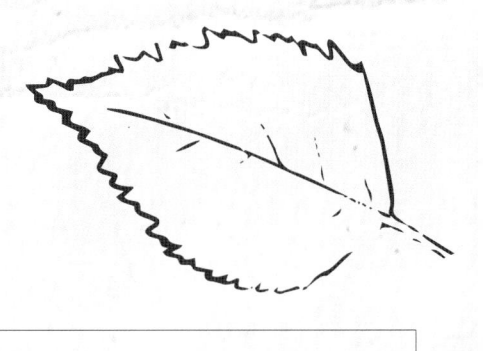

SYNONYM:	*Betula alba* var. *pendula*
NAME ORIGIN:	*Betula* is Latin for birch and *pendula* means pendulous or weeping. *Birce* is the Anglo-Saxon word for birch.
FAMILY:	**Betulaceae**

EDIBLE PART:	Sap
EDIBILITY RATING:	4
WHERE IT'S FOUND:	Deciduous forest.
MONTH SPAN:	Last week of February - 2nd week March.
CAUTIONS:	Avoid if you have heart and kidney problems, or suffer from oedema (fluid build up in the body's tissues).

FOOD IDEAS:	Birch sap wine, birch sap syrup.
OTHER INFO:	To collect the sap, choose a tree that has a diameter of more than 25cm. You need to drill a hole with an auger (hand drill) or using a sturdy sharp knife at an upward angle, about a foot and a half to a metre above the ground and about 3cm deep at a 20 degree angle sloping down from the tree. Unfortunately you are allocated a small window of opportunity to get this right - it is easy to tap too early or too late which causes years (literally!) of disappointment! You can either poke an end of rubber tubing in to the tree as long as it is a tight fit, or fashion a spout from a branch where you can attach the tubing to and the other end into a sealed demi-john (through a hole in the bung) or galvanised covered bucket, otherwise just let it drip freely into a container. Leave for 24 hours and return with your fingers crossed. Remember to block up the hole with a branch that fits well so you don't encourage bacteria or diseases into the tree.
	If you hear about xylitol in mints, pastilles or any dental products it is a sugar alcohol produced from birch and other plants. Xylon means wood in Greek. This is a sugar that has beneficial properties for teeth!

SCALLOPS

Pecten maximus Great scallop
Aequipecten opercularis Queen scallop

NAME ORIGIN:	**Scallop shells are a symbol of the traveller as well as Venus and scallop comes from the French escalope meaning shell.**
FAMILY:	**Pectinidae**
EDIBLE PART:	White meat and orange coral.
EDIBILITY RATING:	5
WHERE IT'S FOUND:	Sea
CAUTIONS:	Allergies to shellfish, collect from clean areas.
MONTH SPAN:	When there is an 'r' in the month.

FOOD IDEAS:	Scallops with black pudding or chorizo, pan fried, steamed with Chinese flavours, added to fish pie or coquilles Saint Jacques where it is served in its own shell topped with mash and a cheese sauce, breadcrumbs and baked.
OTHER INFO:	Santiago otherwise known as St James was one of the apostles along with his brother John (sons of Zebedee!) and both were fishermen. He travelled around the Mediterranean. Unfortunately he was beheaded by Herod and his remains were taken and buried at Compostela (in Spain). Today there are three major pilgrim routes through Europe to Santiago de Compostela, through France and even Cornwall. A few years ago, Dad, Nick and I did a small part of this pilgrimage which took us from St Ives to Marazion, where the monks would have stayed at St Michael's Mount. We all found decent 'staffs' to help us along the way and Dad's is now adorned with a scallop shell on the top! If you are buying scallops, try and choose hand picked not dredged as the dredging process seriously damages the flora and fauna of the sea bed which in turn destroys habitats for other wildlife. Did you know scallops have 100 eyes? Scallops are grown for food in parts of the world by the process called aquaculture.

SCALLOPS WITH CHORIZO AND PEA PUREE

200g frozen peas
1 small sprig of mint
1 tbsp butter
1 tbsp olive oil
6-8 scallops
6-8 slices of chorizo
seasoning

Make the pea puree first by boiling the peas for 3 minutes and drain so they should still have good colour and flavour (not like wet dog). Blitz with the mint and a little seasoning. Grill or pan fry the slices of chorizo until getting colour and crispness (I don't use any oil or fat as they have plenty in them already). Put the oil and butter in a pan and heat until starting to foam, then add the scallops and cook on both sides on a medium heat until golden. I prefer my scallops cooked through but not chewy. On a plate spread a dollop of pea puree across your plate with a palette knife and add the chorizo and scallops. Serve with a little salad of your choice.

PRICKLY SOW THISTLE

Sonchus asper

NAME ORIGIN:	*Asper* means rough, *Sonchus* means hollow and is the ancient Greek name of the plant (it has a hollow stem).
FAMILY:	Asteraceae

EDIBLE PART:	Juicy stems, roots, tender leaves.
EDIBILITY RATING:	3
WHERE IT'S FOUND:	Cultivated ground.
LOOKALIKES:	Other thistle shoots but they are all harmless.
MONTH SPAN:	Flowers June - August, seeds ripen July - September.

FOOD IDEAS:	Eat the young leaves raw or cooked. Peel and eat the stems raw or cooked - it is suggested that the milky sap is washed out of them before eating as this is the bitter part. These make pretty good crudités.
OTHER INFO:	As with sow thistles in general, they are so called as they supposedly help sows lactate.

SOUTHERNWOOD Lad's love
Artemisia abrotanum

NAME ORIGIN:	**Named after Artemis the Greek goddess (also known as Diana) and *abrotanum* is the Latin name for southernwood.**
FAMILY:	**Asteraceae**
EDIBLE PART:	Young shoots
EDIBILITY RATING:	2
WHERE IT'S FOUND:	Dappled shade, hedge.
CAUTIONS:	No reports but some plants in this family have been known to cause dermatitis/allergic reactions. Avoid during pregnancy.
LOOKALIKES:	Other Artemisias.
MONTH SPAN:	(Hz 4) In leaf from March, flowers September - October.

FOOD IDEAS:	Young shoots used as a flavouring (bitter and lemon flavour), tea from shoots. It is quite an acquired taste due to the bitterness. In parts of the Mediterranean such as Italy, it is used as a culinary herb, used for flavouring puddings and desserts.
OTHER INFO:	This plant is mostly used as a moth or insect repellent. In French the plant is called 'garderobe' meaning clothes protector.

CRYSTALLIZED
FLOWERS

To crystallize primrose flowers take an egg white and beat lightly until frothy (not too much as if you are making meringue). Paint it on to the primrose flowers with a fine paint brush and coat with caster sugar. Leave to dry on baking parchment - sprinkle caster sugar on the baking sheet first, then place the sugar-coated flowers on it. They harden and last for a long time, looking beautiful as cake decorations.

PRIMROSE

Primula vulgaris

SYNONYM:	*Primula acaulis*
NAME ORIGIN:	**Primus is Latin for the first (early flowering) and *vulgaris* means common. The name 'primrose' comes from *prime rosa* meaning first rose.**
FAMILY:	**Primulaceae**
EDIBLE PART:	Flowers, leaves raw or cooked.
EDIBILITY RATING:	2
WHERE IT'S FOUND:	Meadow, hedgerow.
LOOKALIKES:	See cautions
CAUTIONS:	Don't try any indoor plants that look like primroses, e.g. *Primula obconica* as handling this plant alone can give an allergic reaction.
MONTH SPAN:	(Hz 6) Flowers December - May.

FOOD IDEAS:	Eat the leaves raw in salads or cooked as a spring leaf vegetable, eat the flowers raw in salads, as a garnish or crystallized - the leaves leave a slight sweet taste in the mouth after eating.
OTHER INFO:	Primroses and violets are the epitome of spring! Harvest sporadically leaving plenty on the plants as over the years their numbers have dropped dramatically due to over collection in over populated areas.

DEAD-NETTLES

Lamium album White dead-nettle
Lamium purpureum Red dead-nettle
Lamium galeobdolon **(subsp. *argentatum*)** Yellow archangel

SYNONYM:	*Lamium galeobdolon* is *Lamiastrum galeobdolon*
NAME ORIGIN:	*Lamium* is Latin for throat, *album* means white, *purpureum* means purple and *galeobdolon* is Greek for smell of a weasel! The subspecies *argentatum* means silver - this is the variegated form of yellow archangel which has silver streaked leaves.
FAMILY:	**Lamiaceae**
EDIBLE PART:	Leaves and flowers from white dead-nettle. Leaves from red dead-nettle. Cooked leaves, roots and flowers from yellow archangel.
EDIBILITY RATING:	2
WHERE IT'S FOUND:	For white dead-nettles: hedge banks, roadsides, waste places. For red dead-nettles: cultivated ground. For yellow archangel: shade, hedgerows, woodland edges.
LOOKALIKES:	Nettles (*Urtica dioica*) can look like dead-nettle but - nettles sting, dead-nettles don't! Nettles don't flower in the same way but produce tiny flowers and seed pods.
MONTH SPAN:	Flowers from March - December. Flowers from March - October. Flowers from May - June.
OTHER INFO:	For A level art, our 2 art teachers took our little art group to Ruthin in North Wales to stay in a tiny freezing cottage with no running water, but we did have jenga to keep us occupied. We would go out into the barren heath landscape and sketch, draw and paint all day. One of the art teachers was passing from one of us to another, critiquing our work, and strangely her main comment would be 'It's quite dark - I think you need to lighten it'. When she came to me, sure enough she said - 'It's quite dark…'. I looked at her and said 'could it be your shades?…'. Just outside the cottage was a massive patch of white dead-nettle - I was really in to hedgerow medicines and this one was one that is good as a general anti-inflammatory and mild sedative. You can drink the nectar from the white flowers too.

Yellow archangel

White dead-nettle

Red dead-nettle

FOOD IDEAS:

White dead-nettle: raw or cooked leaves, flowers taste good, cook the aerial parts before flowering as a vegetable. The leaves are best when they are young or before they flower.
Red dead-nettle: eat the young shoots.
Yellow archangel: eat the young flower tips, leaves and young stems cooked.

Not worth a recipe unfortunately as I think some will find this very bitter. Pick the new growth without any flowers or flower buds. Wash well and steam with water and serve with a little melted butter. They taste quite similar to nettles (almost hoppy) but can be too bitter for some. Did I mention about tasters and non-tasters? A small percentage of the population can't taste certain bitter compounds and this could explain why a fair chunk of people don't like Brussels sprouts as they contain these bitter compounds (could also be the overcooked slop we were given at school). This small percentage of non tasters have a much wider repertoire of foods they can eat but a downside for our ancestors would have been they were more likely to eat something toxic and not know about it!

SWEET VIOLET
Viola odorata

DOG VIOLET
Viola riviniana

NAME ORIGIN:	*Viola* is the ancient Latin name for a violet, *odorata* means scented.
FAMILY:	Violaceae
EDIBLE PART:	Flowers, leaves.
EDIBILITY RATING:	2
WHERE IT'S FOUND:	Pastures, hedgerows, woods.
MONTH SPAN:	*Viola odorata* flowers February - April. *Viola riviniana* flowers March - June.

FOOD IDEAS:	Crystallize the flowers. The flowers and leaves can be used to thicken soups.
OTHER INFO:	In repressed Victorian times, people would show their true feelings by giving bouquets to one another in secret - the flowers each with its own meaning. This was called The Language of Flowers. Violets represent retiring modesty after the Greek mythology of Viola, a nymph who was constantly pursued by Apollo so Diana turned her into a violet to protect her. The Language of Flowers isn't always for seduction… geraniums can mean stupidity and narcissus means you think too much of yourself (narcissist)!

CRYSTALLIZED VIOLETS

Crystallize the flowers by beating egg whites, painting onto the flowers and dip in caster sugar. Shake off excess and leave to dry on a baking tray in a warm dry place. Once dried, they can be stored in an airtight container and they last a long time.

RAMSONS
Bear leek (old name)

Allium ursinum

NAME ORIGIN:	*All* is Celtic for burning and pungent and *ursa* means bear in Latin, hence the name bear leek. This was used as a culinary herb until garlic was introduced from the Mediterranean. The Egyptians raised it to God status!
FAMILY:	Amaryllidaceae
EDIBLE PART:	Leaves (flowers later, then unripe seed pods).
EDIBILITY RATING:	5
WHERE IT'S FOUND:	Shady banks, hedgerows, deciduous woodland.
CAUTIONS:	Possibly toxic to dogs.
LOOKALIKES:	It can look like Lords and Ladies (*Arum* sp.) and other spring leaves coming up but rip a piece of leaf and smell - if you can't smell garlic, then it is not ramsons.
MONTH SPAN:	(Hz 5) In leaf from February, flowers May - June, seeds ripen May - July.

FOOD IDEAS:	There are so many food ideas and recipes - as a filling for nettle or spinach roulade, soup, pesto, pickled unripe ramson seed pods, the flowers are almost hot with pungency, whereas 3 cornered leek is a milder flavour - can you take it?! The bulbs are also excellent as a garlic bulb substitute but remember you have to get the landowner's permission and if you don't dig it up, you get much more foliage, flowers etc to come back year after year. Use them as dolmades to replace vine leaves, wild garlic pesto or one of my favourites wild garlic bread by mixing it with butter, thyme and rosemary and spread it in the crevices of a multi-sliced baguette and bake in the oven nestled in a foil hammock until golden.
OTHER INFO:	Found in shady hedgerows, banks and deciduous woods, this is an unmistakable prolific plant from the onion and garlic family. If in doubt, snap a leaf off and have a good sniff! Either use its broad long floppy green leaves or its white star like flowers in your cooking as both give a fantastic pungent garlicky flavour.

RAMSONS GARLIC BREAD

some sort of bread
(baguette is best)
15 washed ramson leaves
3 tbsp butter
a glug of olive oil
sea salt
ground black pepper
optional to add herbs such as
rosemary and thyme

This has to be the recipe for ramson garlic bread… absolutely delicious! Either bake your own bread or baguette or buy it and make it taste amazing! Finely shred the ramson leaves and add to a bowl with all of the ingredients. Mash together with a fork. Make incisions 3/4 of the way through the baguette and spread the mixture into the cuts (or just spread onto the bread). Bake in the oven at 180 degrees C for about 10 mins in a tin foil nest (open at the top) until the bread is turning golden and crusty and the ramson butter has melted.

OH SO GREEN! PASTA

4 handfuls of farfalle pasta
1 sliced courgette
3 - 4 chopped broccoli florets
20-30 green beans
1 tub mascarpone
2 handfuls of ramson leaves
olive oil for frying
salt and pepper for seasoning

Bring enough water to the boil to cook the pasta and steam the broccoli and green beans over it. Heat about a tbsp of olive oil in a frying pan and add the courgette slices until golden on both sides. When the pasta, broccoli and beans are done, add them to the frying pan, stir in the mascarpone, finely chop the ramsons and add, remove from the heat, taste and season accordingly.

GARLIC MUSTARD

Jack by the hedge

Alliaria petiolata

NAME ORIGIN:	The genus probably means 'like an *Allium*' as it smells like garlic but is in the mustard (Brassica) family. *Petiolata* means a leaf with a stalk.
FAMILY:	**Brassicaceae**
EDIBLE PART:	Young leaves, flowers and seed pods.
EDIBILITY RATING:	4
WHERE IT'S FOUND:	Hedgerows, woodland edge.
MONTH SPAN:	Flowers April to June, biennial with overwintering basal leaves. Seeds ripen June - August.

FOOD IDEAS:	The delicious leaves have a garlicky mustard flavour - chop plenty of leaves and mix in to mash served with sausages, toad in the hole or bubble and squeak. Tastes better before it flowers as it goes bitter.
OTHER INFO:	When cooked it has a very delicate flavour so add more fresh leaves if you like it to taste stronger.

LAMB CUTLETS WITH GARLIC MUSTARD SALSA VERDE

lamb cutlets
olive oil
handfuls of garlic mustard
seasoning

Wash and finely chop the garlic mustard, and keep half for the salsa verde and put the other half in a bowl, along with a good slug of olive oil, seasoning and the lamb cutlets, rubbing them around in the flavours. Cover in cling film and pop in the fridge to infuse. Pan fry the lamb for 20 minutes turning frequently to cook each side. For the salsa verde put the remaining garlic mustard in a bowl, add a drizzle of olive oil and spoon over the cutlets. Serve with mash (with garlic mustard stirred through?) and a simple salad (with garlic mustard in?!).

NAVELWORT Pennywort
Umbilicus rupestris

SYNONYM:	*Umbilicus pedulinus, Cotyledon umbilicus-veneris*
NAME ORIGIN:	*Umbilicus* means belly button and *rupestris* means ruptured or swollen, in other words rupturing bellybutton! Nice! This is what it looks like, not what it does!
FAMILY:	**Crassulaceae**

EDIBLE PART:	Leaves
EDIBILITY RATING:	2
WHERE IT'S FOUND:	Any walls and rocky crevices.
LOOKALIKES:	The genus *Saxifraga* is most similar but these mostly have rosette-shaped foliage whereas navelwort is a simple fleshy disc and grows in abundance.
MONTH SPAN:	All year round.

FOOD IDEAS:	Eat the leaves as a wayside snack, in sandwiches instead of cucumber (although it doesn't taste as good as cucumber) or try frying it - it tastes a little inky which is quite pleasant.
OTHER INFO:	Use as a temperate *Aloe* for cooling grazes. This plant is very prolific in the South West of the British Isles and can even be found growing on mossy trees.

CROCUS

Crocus sp.

NAME ORIGIN:	The Greek word *krokos* means saffron, from the word *kroke* meaning thread relating to the thread-like filaments of the styles (female thread-like part with stigma at the tip) which is the source of the dye *(Crocus sativus)*. Related to meadow saffron, Colchis in classical mythology was a place famed for its medicinal plants.
FAMILY:	Iridaceae

EDIBLE PART:	Stigma
EDIBILITY RATING:	1
WHERE IT'S FOUND:	Meadows, dappled shade.
CAUTIONS:	Only use the style and stigma in food, most croci flower in spring, saffron crocus flowers September-October. Unfortunately colchicums flower mostly in autumn too and are poisonous - see lookalikes for how to spot the difference. Abortifacient and emmenagogue.
LOOKALIKES:	*Colchicum* sp. look like *Crocus* sp. and are poisonous. Common names are very misleading as 'autumn crocus' are *Colchicum* sp. and an 'autumn flowering crocus' is a *Crocus*. *Crocus* sp. have 3 stamen (male flower parts) and flat papery corms where *Colchicum* sp. have 6 stamen with irregular waxy leathery brown corms.
MONTH SPAN:	Most croci flower in spring, saffron crocus flowers September - October

FOOD IDEAS:	Use the style and stigma (female flower parts) as a yellow food dye for rice, cakes, puddings, especially saffron buns - a true Cornish speciality!
OTHER INFO:	Saffron is one of the most expensive 'spices' weight for weight, more expensive than gold.

SEA KALE
Crambe maritima

NAME ORIGIN:	*Crambe* is the Greek name for cabbage and *maritima* means maritime or sea coast.
FAMILY:	**Brassicaceae**
EDIBLE PART:	Leaves, flower buds, stems.
EDIBILITY RATING:	5
WHERE IT'S FOUND:	Mostly shingle beaches on the south coast.
MONTH SPAN:	Flowers June - August. Perennial (Hz 5).

FOOD IDEAS:	Use it in quiche, as a vegetable, raw or cooked or shredded. Treat this vegetable as you would cabbage or purple sprouting broccoli so as a vegetable try it steamed, boiled, poached in milk, stir fried, as a soup. If you are lucky enough to live near shingle coastlines where this grows, as you see the sea kale emerging, bury the new shoots with a pile of stones to exclude the light. This way you are forcing it like you would rhubarb and in a couple of weeks, uncover and harvest the long pale shoots, simmer until tender and serve with melted butter to dip in. Later in the year try eating the raw flower buds, honey-like flowers and unripe seed pods.
OTHER INFO:	We have a horticultural show here in Cornwall called the Boconnoc Spring Garden Show for which I have done many displays and show gardens for several years. A few years ago we did 'The Incredible Seashore' which my mate Gill designed as she has a romantic connection to the sea, water, swimming and especially the Scillies. We accumulated many maritime plants from all over, especially an excellent nursery called 'Naturescape' which is incredible - they managed to source *Eryngium maritimum* for us, plus many other plants. Sea kale was one we managed to get hold of (all legitimately I promise!!) and I now have it in my garden and have got to try it for the first time! It tends to grow in shingle, especially on beaches along the south coast of England, but not so much in Cornwall. It's delicious, just like broccoli or cabbage. Serve as a vegetable as it really holds its own, or put it in a quiche (Nick's favourite ever meal is broccoli and tuna quiche so this is one I'll be testing on him!).

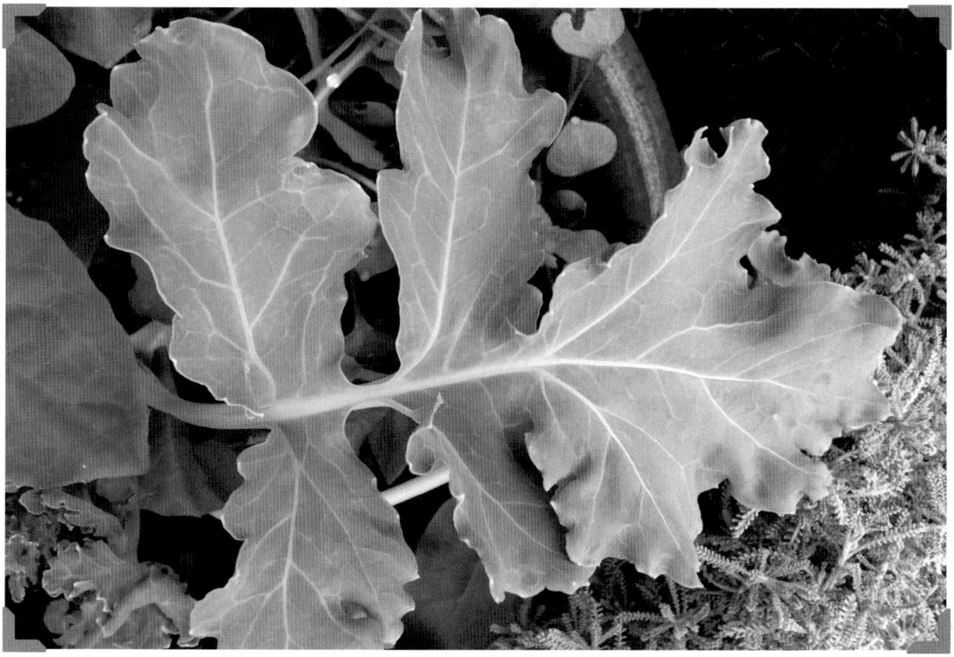

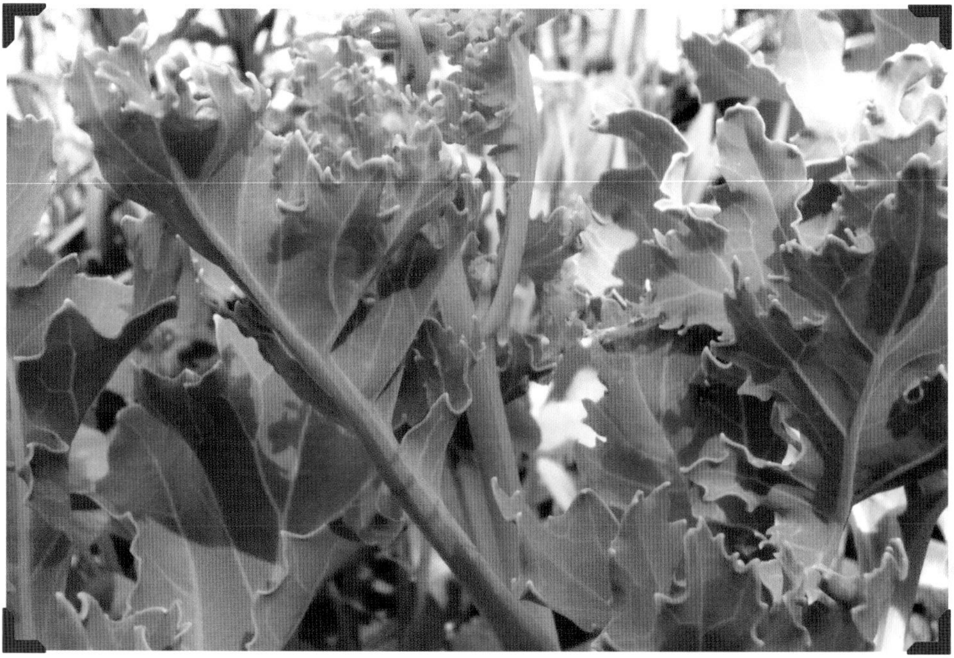

ORACHE
(Atriplex hastata - spear-leaved orache)
Atriplex sp.

NAME ORIGIN:	The Greek *a* means no and *traphein* means nourishment as it grows in poor soil.
FAMILY:	Chenopodiaceae

EDIBLE PART:	Leaves
EDIBILITY RATING:	2
WHERE IT'S FOUND:	Muddy estuaries, sand, coastal, waste ground.
LOOKALIKES:	The difference between *Atriplex* and *Chenopodium* is that *Chenopodium* sp. have 'perfect' or 'bi-sexual' flowers meaning their flowers have both male and female parts, where *Atriplex* sp. have 'uni-sexual' flowers. Quite hard to see with the naked eye but *Chenopodium* and *Atriplex* are so closely related I wouldn't worry too much about it!
MONTH SPAN:	Flowers July - September.
CAUTIONS:	The only caution is due to what the plant is growing in (fertilisers used on crops) as they can absorb nitrates.

FOOD IDEAS:	Eat it as a vegetable with other greens or in a soup. I don't think the flavour holds its own.

HAWTHORN
Crataegus monogyna

NAME ORIGIN:	The Greek *krataigos* means flowering thorn (*kratos* means strength). *Monogyna* means single pistil.
FAMILY:	**Rosaceae**

EDIBLE PART:	Young leaves, flowers (for the fruits (haws) see Oct 23rd).
EDIBILITY RATING:	2
WHERE IT'S FOUND:	Hedgerows, woodland, thickets.
MONTH SPAN:	Flowers May - June, fruits ripen September - November.

FOOD IDEAS:	Young tender leaves are good in salads (slightly nutty, dry flavour and texture, although I loath to use the word 'nutty' as it is overused!). The flowers are also edible.
OTHER INFO:	It is a tonic for the heart and reduces high blood pressure. Eating the raw leaves, leaves a slightly sweet, almost jasmine like after taste. Hawthorn is also called 'May' and it is very bad luck to bring the blossom into the home as it is associated with illness and death, the reason being the flowers contain trimethylamine which is also present in decaying animal tissue! When the flowers start to go over, they have been described as smelling like the great plague of London.

CRAB APPLE
Malus sylvestris

SYNONYM:	*Malus acerba, Malus communis* **var.** *sylvestris, Pyrus malus*
NAME ORIGIN:	*Malus* **is Latin for apple tree and** *sylvestris* **means woodland.**
FAMILY:	**Rosaceae**
EDIBLE PART:	Flowers (leaves in small quantities - see cautions) (for the apples see Oct 27th).
EDIBILITY RATING:	3
WHERE IT'S FOUND:	Sunny or dappled hedgerows or woodland (especially oak).
CAUTIONS:	Hydrogen cyanide in leaves and seeds, not in the fruit. Small doses are fine.
LOOKALIKES:	Other trees in the Rosaceae family such as pears which have white flowers whereas apple blossom has a pink tinge to it.
MONTH SPAN:	(Hz 4) Flowers March, fruits ripen September - October.

FOOD IDEAS:	Crystallize the flowers, make spring blossom cordial.
OTHER INFO:	Apples have always been a symbol of love, for instance apple peel thrown over your shoulder would land in the shape of a letter (or something resembling perhaps) which your future husband's name would begin with. If you cut an apple across the centre, you reveal a pentagon of pips - the pentagram has been a symbol used in many beliefs and religions, from the mathematical perfect of Pythagoras' theorem, the Chinese Wu Xing where the 5 points represent the 5 elements wood, fire, earth, metal and water, Christianity with the 5 wounds of Christ on the cross and with Paganism and the Occult with the point facing up to the 'heavens' or spirit with the 4 elements.

LARCH
Larix decidua

SYNONYM:	*Larix europaea*
NAME ORIGIN:	*Larix* is the old Latin name and *decidua* means deciduous as this is one of the UK's deciduous conifers.
FAMILY:	Pinaceae

EDIBLE PART:	Inner bark and manna.
EDIBILITY RATING:	I
WHERE IT'S FOUND:	Forests and woodlands.
CAUTIONS:	Contains galactose so avoid if lactose intolerant, avoid if you have allergies, avoid inhalation as it can inflame airways and it can cause kidney failure.
MONTH SPAN:	Flowers April - May, seeds October - November.

FOOD IDEAS:	Inner bark dried and ground to a powder to make bread.
OTHER INFO:	Larch wood is pretty useful as it can be used for boat building as it copes well with changes in saturation from wet to dry. It also produces turpentine (I love the smell of turpentine in the morning).

DAISY
Bellis perennis

NAME ORIGIN:	*Bellis* is Latin for pretty and *perennis* means perennial.
FAMILY:	Asteraceae

EDIBLE PART:	Leaves and flowers.
EDIBILITY RATING:	2
WHERE IT'S FOUND:	Any grassland, including lawns.
CAUTIONS:	It is best to avoid if pregnant.
MONTH SPAN:	Flowers and foliage are available all year round.

FOOD IDEAS:	Daisy flowers are more decorative than anything, the leaves are ok raw but better cooked and the younger ones taste better as they get a bit tough when they get older. The flowers really don't taste of much at all.
OTHER INFO:	Ahhhh daisy chains! Daisies are useful for a whole list of complaints, especially coughs and colds, skin inflammations and rashes.

ROSEBAY WILLOWHERB Fireweed

Epilobium angustifolium

SYNONYM:	*Chamaenerion angustifolium*
NAME ORIGIN:	*Epi* in Greek means upon and *lobos* means lobe, referring to the petals being situated above the ovary. *Angustifolia* means narrow leaved.
FAMILY:	Onagraceae

EDIBLE PART:	Young (leafy) shoots (For the roots see Sept 5th).
EDIBILITY RATING:	4
WHERE IT'S FOUND:	Waste ground, gardens, woodlands.
CAUTIONS:	Beware of herbicide (or any chemical) spraying as it is an invasive weed.
MONTH SPAN:	Shoots appear in late March, flowers July - September, seeds ripen August - October.

FOOD IDEAS:	Try the young red stemmed shoots steamed or boiled for 5 minutes until tender and served with homemade hollandaise sauce, delicious!
OTHER INFO:	The leaves are meant to stupefy a person, if drunk as an infusion - this may explain a lot!! After fires such as forest fires and bombing such as during WW2 in the Blitz, rosebay willowherb was one of the first plants to grow, hence the name 'fireweed'.

HOMEMADE HOLLANDAISE SAUCE

2 tbsp butter
2 egg yolks
2 tbsp lemon juice
sea salt and black pepper
olive oil optional

In a bowl over simmering water (don't let the bowl touch the water if you can help it) melt the butter and stir in the lemon juice. Using a balloon whisk, add the egg yolks and gently whisk to keep the sauce moving. As it starts to thicken which you'll see when it starts to coat the sides of the bowl, take it off the heat (mind the steam). Season to taste and I sometimes whisk in a little olive oil to make it go further and keep it silky. Steam the washed rosebay willowherb shoots and serve with the hollandaise to dip them in.

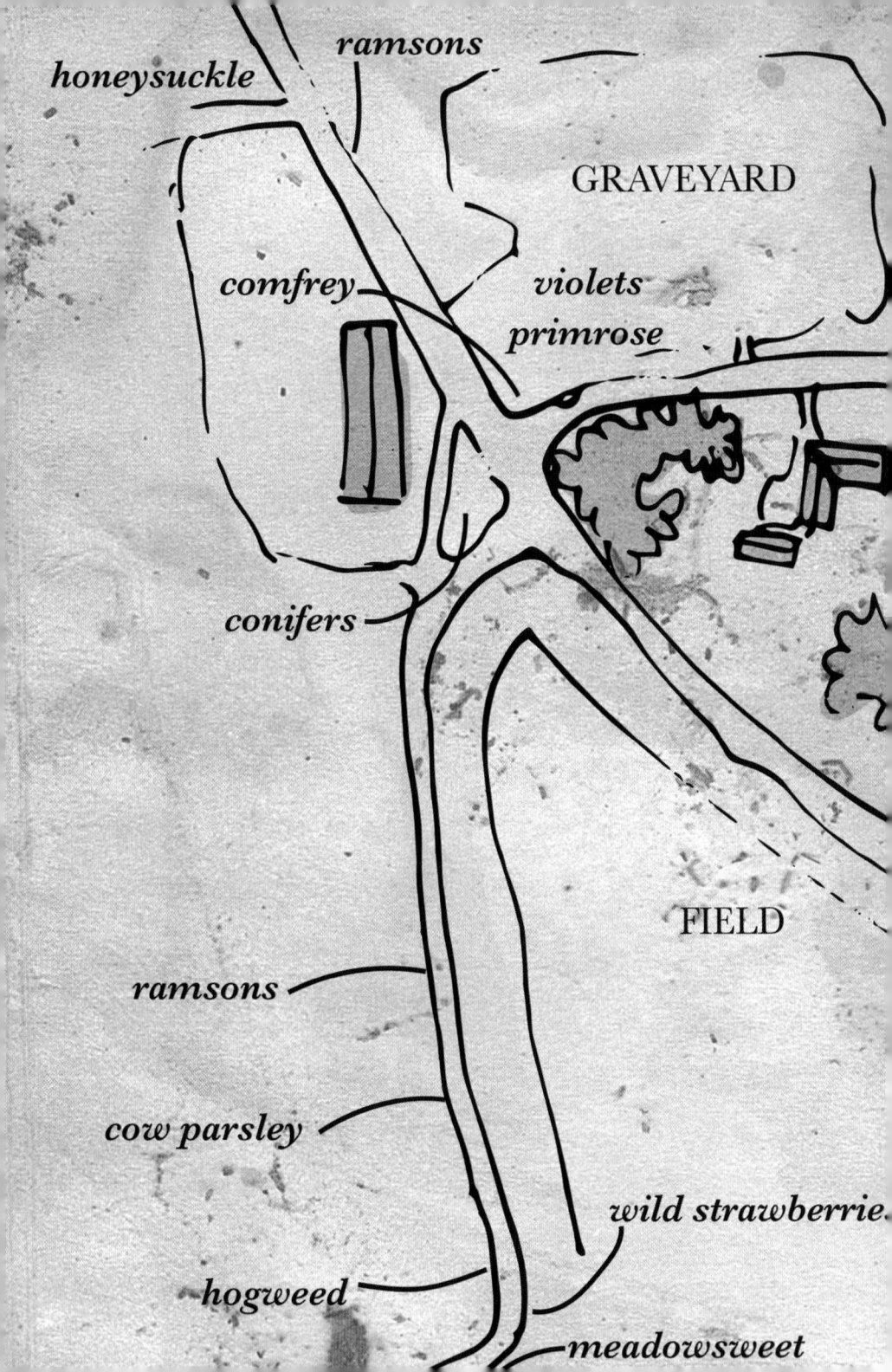

WATERMINT
Mentha aquatica

SYNONYM:	*Mentha hirsuta*
NAME ORIGIN:	Menthe was the name of a Greek nymph who was transformed into the sweet-smelling plant by Persephone. The word *aquatica* means water or living in water in Latin.
FAMILY:	Lamiaceae

EDIBLE PART:	Leaves
EDIBILITY RATING:	4
WHERE IT'S FOUND:	Streams, ponds, rivers, fens, bog
CAUTIONS:	The essential oil of the mint family can cause abortions.
LOOKALIKES:	Other plants in the Lamiaceae family - rub and sniff, you'll soon know whether it is mint or not!
MONTH SPAN:	Flowers July – October, in leaf from about April.

FOOD IDEAS:	Tea from fresh or dried leaves, leaves eaten raw or cooked and used as a flavouring for sweet and savoury dishes.
OTHER INFO:	This is a good palate cleanser or light pudding after a heavy meal. Mint is a cooling herb and menthols (found in mints - the cooling part) are good at stimulating hair growth and relieving indigestion.

WATERMINT SORBET

1 oz watermint leaves
2 lemons
4 oz sugar
1 egg white
3/4 pint of water

Put the water and sugar into a saucepan and zest the lemons into the liquid (you can do strips of it as you'll be sieving it out). Simmer until the sugar has dissolved and continue to heat for an extra 5 minutes. Remove from the heat and add the juice of the lemons and roughly chop the mint and add that too. Leave to infuse and cool - you can leave it overnight if you have the time. When completely cool, sieve out the lemon zest and mint leaves then pop in the freezer for 2-3 hours. Whisk the egg white until stiff. Take the ice mix out of the freezer and blitz it in a food processor or mash up well with a fork. Whisk the ice mix and gently add the egg white, whisking a bit at a time. Freeze. To serve, take out of the freezer about 5-10 minutes before serving.

SIMPLE BAMBOO BROTH

A simple noodle broth works well with bamboo shoots for a little crunch. Prepare the bamboo shoots first by peeling away any sheath and rinse off any irritating hairs. Slice and boil for 5 minutes, rinse and repeat. Meanwhile cook your noodles in stock, and add anything you like for example peas, spring onions, garlic, ginger, chillies, etc. When the noodles are cooked, add all the ingredients to the noodle broth, season with soya sauce, a squeeze of lime or whatever suits your palate.

BLACK BAMBOO

Phyllostachys nigra

NAME ORIGIN:	The word *phyllo* is Greek for leaf, *stachys* means column and *nigra* means black.
FAMILY:	Poaceae

EDIBLE PART:	Young shoots
EDIBILITY RATING:	2
WHERE IT'S FOUND:	Dappled shade, garden escapee
LOOKALIKES:	Other bamboos but no others have black stems.
MONTH SPAN:	Shoots appear from March.

FOOD IDEAS:	Eat the young shoots cooked changing the water once.
OTHER INFO:	Bamboos are excellent architectural plants but you must restrict their roots when planting as they spread like wildfire. Bamboo is so versatile and with its hollow sections it is one of the strongest building materials, architectural bio-mimicry uses it for earthquake proof housing.

HOARY CRESS white top

Cardaria draba

SYNONYM:	*Lepidium draba*
NAME ORIGIN:	The word *kardia* means heart (possibly Greek) referring to the shape of the silicles (Brassica pods). *Draba* is the old Greek name for cress.
FAMILY:	Brassicaceae
EDIBLE PART:	Leaves, roots, seeds, flower heads
EDIBILITY RATING:	3
WHERE IT'S FOUND:	Arable land, cultivated ground, field escapee
CAUTIONS:	The young leaves contain hydrogen cyanide but in small quantities it is harmless.
MONTH SPAN:	Flowers May - June, (Hz 6).

FOOD IDEAS:	Raw or cooked leaves and shoots, the green seeds can be used as a spice or condiment. Fry the leaves in a little butter until crispy, boil or steam the flower buds like broccoli.
OTHER INFO:	This is a fast spreading invasive plant - if you eat it you're helping to control it! With my van, we adapted the inside to make it a mini camper with kitchenette and pull out sofa bed - very impressive! We decided to take it out for a day trip to look for good places to camp and found a lovely spot between Constantine bay on the North coast and Treyarnon. This was where I spotted this unusual plant in mass which smelled and looked like a brassica but nothing I'd ever seen before. Having identified it, this may be one of my new camping spots with plenty to eat!!

FIELD MILK THISTLE

Sonchus arvensis

NAME ORIGIN:	*Sonchus* comes from the Greek word meaning hollow referring to the hollow stems and *arvensis* means of the fields in Latin.
FAMILY:	**Asteraceae**
EDIBLE PART:	Juicy stems, roots, tender leaves
EDIBILITY RATING:	2
WHERE IT'S FOUND:	Cultivated ground, meadow
LOOKALIKES:	Other thistles look similar but they are all safe to eat, some more bitter or prickly than others.
MONTH SPAN:	Flowers July - October, seeds ripen August - October.

FOOD IDEAS:	Roots can be roasted to make coffee and the leaves can be eaten - you may need to cut off the spiny leaf edges. Many sow thistles can be eaten as crudités although some are more bitter than others.
OTHER INFO:	The bitter compounds found in various plants including thistles help stimulate digestive juices in the stomach which aid digestion.

SWEET ALYSSUM
Lobularia maritima

SYNONYM	*Alyssum maritimum, Clypeola maritima*
NAME ORIGIN:	*Lobularia* is Greek for small pod and *maritima* means maritime. The common name *Alyssum* comes from the Greek *a* which means against (or no) and *lyssa* means madness as it was once used to cure madness.
FAMILY:	**Brassicaceae**

EDIBLE PART:	Flowers, aerial parts
EDIBILITY RATING:	3
WHERE IT'S FOUND:	Coastal sandy soil
MONTH SPAN:	In leaf from April, flowers June - October, seeds ripen July - October.

FOOD IDEAS:	Aerial parts can be eaten in salads to give a little bite. The little delicate white flowers add heat to any food and work well as a garnish.

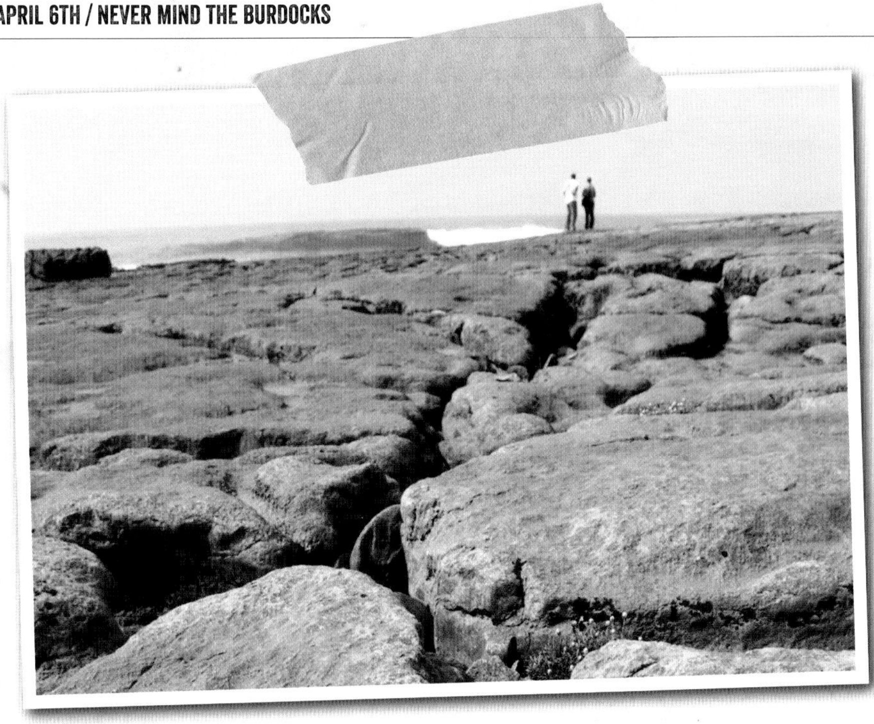

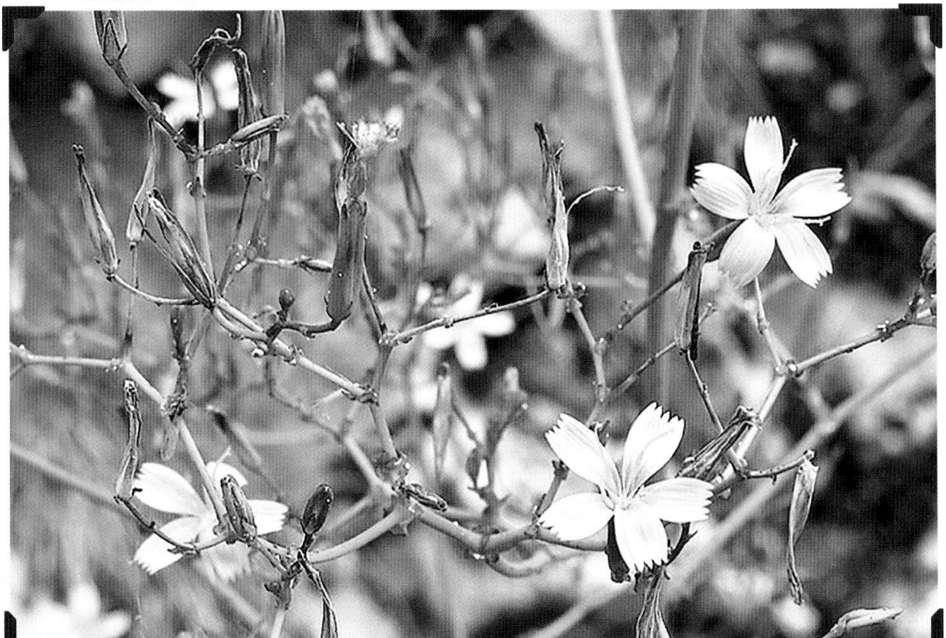

WALL LETTUCE
Mycelis muralis

SYNONYM:	*Lactuca muralis, Prenanthes muralis*
NAME ORIGIN:	The species name *muralis* comes from *murus* which is Latin for wall. The synonym *Lactuca* comes from the word *lac* meaning milk in Latin as it exudes a milky sap.
FAMILY:	Asteraceae

EDIBLE PART:	Leaves
EDIBILITY RATING:	2
WHERE IT'S FOUND:	Shady walls, road sides, beech woods
LOOKALIKES:	Quite closely related to chicory *Cinchorum intybus* except wall lettuce has 5 little yellow petals as opposed to chicory's blue multi-petalled flowers.
MONTH SPAN:	Flowers July - September.

FOOD IDEAS:	Eat the raw leaves in salads.
OTHER INFO:	Wall lettuce grows abundantly in The Burren, a stunning landscape of layered, fissured limestone in County Clare, worth visiting in the spring when there is a rich tapestry of wild flowers including gentians and wild orchids.

WILD PEAR
Pyrus communis

NAME ORIGIN:	*Pyrus* is the classic name for pear tree, *communis* means common or communities.
FAMILY:	Rosaceae
EDIBLE PART:	Flowers (for fruit see November 30th)
EDIBILITY RATING:	3
WHERE IT'S FOUND:	Hedges, woodlands
CAUTIONS:	Hydrogen cyanide in leaves and seeds, not in the fruit. Small doses are fine.
LOOKALIKES:	Other trees in the Rosaceae family look similar. Pears have white flowers whereas apple blossom has a pink tinge to it.
MONTH SPAN:	Flowers April - May, fruits ripen October - December.

FOOD IDEAS:	Eat the flowers, use as a garnish or as a delicate flavouring. Why not try making pear blossom cordial? Pick the best looking blossoms ideally when it is dry and sunny and use the same recipe as for elderflower cordial, substituting elder blossoms for pear.
OTHER INFO:	Pears have been around for a long time, possibly dating back to neolithic and bronze age.

EASTER LEDGE PUDDING

300g bistort leaves
100g nettle tops
(other spring edible
leaves can be added)
1 onion or
a handful of ramson leaves
100g pearl/pot barley
25g oatmeal
1 egg
1 dessertspoon melted
butter
seasoning
oil or butter to fry

There are many variations on this dish, not to mention the World Dock Pudding Championships held in Mytholmroyd in West Yorkshire every year! Here is one way of cooking it.

Finely chop the greens and onion (or ramsons). Mix well with the barley, season and wrap tightly in a muslin cloth and simmer in a saucepan of water for 2 hours. Unwrap the barley mix and tip into a bowl, mixing in the beaten egg and melted butter until thoroughly combined. Stir through the oatmeal, roll into little cakes and fry in the oil or butter in a frying pan until golden on both sides.

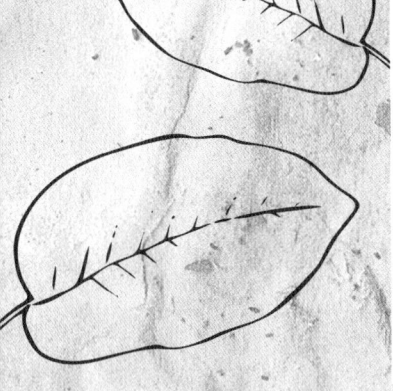

BISTORT

Easter ledge   pudding grass   adderwort   patient dock
dragonwort   Easter giant   passion dock   snakeweed
gentle dock   pink pokers   red legs

Polygonum bistorta

SYNONYM:	*Persicaria bistorta*
NAME ORIGIN:	*Polygonum* means many joints (or knees!) and the common name bistort comes from the Latin *bistorta*, referring to the twisted shape of the plant's rhizome (root).
FAMILY:	Polygonaceae
EDIBLE PART:	Leaves
EDIBILITY RATING:	2
WHERE IT'S FOUND:	Damp soil, near water, damp meadows
CAUTIONS:	Can cause possible photosensitivity and it contains oxalic acid so avoid if you have rheumatism, arthritis, etc.
MONTH SPAN:	(Hz 4) Perennial, flowers June - September, seeds ripen August - October.
FOOD IDEAS:	Bistort is the main ingredient for Easter ledge pudding, made from an assortment of other edible leaves, pearl barley and made into little cakes and fried.

BLACK MUSTARD
Brassica nigra

SYNONYM:	*Sinapis nigra, Brassica brachycarpa, Brassica sinapioides, Sisymbrium nigrum*
NAME ORIGIN:	The word *Brassica* comes from the Celtic word bresic meaning cabbage, *nigra* means black.
FAMILY:	Brassicaceae

EDIBLE PART:	Leaves raw or cooked, stems (for seeds see Aug 28th)
EDIBILITY RATING:	4
WHERE IT'S FOUND:	Coastal and inland waste ground
CAUTIONS:	Seeds and oil can be an irritant, especially for children.
LOOKALIKES:	With their 4 petalled yellow flowers, many in the mustard family look alike, but they are pretty much all edible. *Brassica nigra* has rough-to-the-touch leaves like I imagine elephant skin feels.
MONTH SPAN:	In leaf almost all year round, flowers June - August, seeds ripen July - September.

FOOD IDEAS:	This has an amazing pungent mustard flavour making it a good addition to a ham sandwich! Use in salads, soups, stews, raw or cooked.
OTHER INFO:	Years ago I made a warm lavender and mustard foot bath to relieve aching tired feet - the mustard really warms the foot and soothes aches and pains. Black mustard helps aid conception and childbirth.

SUSHI AND BLACK MUSTARD

Black mustard tastes very similar to wasabi with its warm, sweet and mustard-hot taste which is delicious.

Cook up your sushi rice as instructed on the packet - brown sushi rice seems to take a bit longer than white sushi rice and there's debate on whether it should be soaked for 1/2 an hour first, or just washed and brought to the boil, simmering from cold.

sushi rice
sushi nori sheets
1 tbsp rice wine vinegar
1 tbsp mirin
A good pinch of sea salt
1 tsp sugar
black mustard leaves
fillings of your choice
soya sauce
pickled ginger

With all sushi rice, the rice is left to steam to absorb all the water. When ready, add a tbsp of rice wine vinegar (white wine vinegar can be used too), a tbsp of mirin if you have it, then add the sea salt and sugar. Stir well and decide on fillings - this can be avocado, raw salmon, mackerel or tuna, tinned tuna, spring onions, cucumber, omelette and combine 2 or 3 if you wish. Wash young black mustard leaves and cut into thin ribbons. Compile your rice and fillings on the sushi nori (seaweed sheet) and lay a few strips of black mustard leaf along the centre. Roll up, wet to seal, slice into rounds and munch with soya sauce and pickled ginger - ooooooo!

SMOOTH SOW THISTLE

Sonchus oleraceus

NAME ORIGIN:	*Sonchus* is Latin for hollow referring to the hollow stem, *oleraceus* loosely means tasty edible vegetable.
FAMILY:	**Asteraceae**

EDIBLE PART:	Leaves raw or cooked, juicy stems (peeled) and roots
EDIBILITY RATING:	3
WHERE IT'S FOUND:	Sunny, cultivated ground, roadsides
LOOKALIKES:	Other similar looking thistles but all are safe to eat.
MONTH SPAN:	Flowers June - August, seeds ripen July - September.

FOOD IDEAS:	The stems can be eaten as crudités, eat the cooked roots, try the leaves in salads.
OTHER INFO:	The taste can really vary from juicy and sweet to bitter. This has the best tasting leaves out of all the thistles and Maoris ate the dried sap like chewing gum.

PERENNIAL WALL ROCKET

Diplotaxis tenuifolia

SYNONYM:	*Brassica tenuifolia, Sisymbrium tenuifolium*
NAME ORIGIN:	The Greek word *diplo* means double, *taxis* means 'line' which refers to the double row of seeds in their pods and *tenuifolia* means narrow leaved. .
FAMILY:	**Brassicaceae**
EDIBLE PART:	Leaves, flowers
EDIBILITY RATING:	4
WHERE IT'S FOUND:	Waste places, old walls, can cope with coastal conditions
LOOKALIKES:	Ragwort *Senecio jacobaea* and groundsel *Senecio vulgaris* leaves are similar but wall rocket has much more delicate leaves, and the flowers are typically brassica-shaped with 4 petals; the old family name was Cruciferae, referring to the cross shape made by the 4 petals.
MONTH SPAN:	Flowers May - September, seeds ripen June - October.
FOOD IDEAS:	Perennial wall rocket has a real warming bite to it! I've started to see it everywhere, even in a pub car park at the base of a wall, growing amongst cobbles!

WALL ROCKET PESTO

This is my second most favourite pesto recipe (I detest basil pesto although love all the components of it - weird).

3 - 4 good handfuls of wall rocket
2 cups of toasted flaked almonds
1 large garlic clove chopped
a good pinch of sea salt
black pepper
olive oil

In a food processor, put in all of the ingredients except the olive oil and blend. Check it has blended fairly well, scraping down the sides back to the bottom, then turn on again. Whilst running, pour the olive oil in until it is the consistency you like. Have it as a dip, with pasta, on potatoes, with chicken…

HONESTY
Lunaria annua

SYNONYM:	*Lunaria biennis*
NAME ORIGIN:	The Latin word *luna* means moon, referring to the shape and silvery colour of the seed pods.
FAMILY:	**Brassicaceae**

EDIBLE PART:	Flowers and leaves, seedlings, seeds
EDIBILITY RATING:	2
WHERE IT'S FOUND	Moist soils, full sun or semi-shade, road sides
MONTH SPAN:	(hz 6) Flowers April - July, seeds ripen June - August

FOOD IDEAS:	The flowers are a beautiful shade of purple, and are a good addition to salads, as are the young leaves. The root is at its best in winter and can be eaten raw or cooked. The seedlings can be eaten like alfalfa sprouts. The ground-up seeds when soaked in cold water for 10 minutes increase the heat and flavour, which can be used as a mustard-like condiment.
OTHER INFO:	The papery seed cases are used in dried flower arranging.

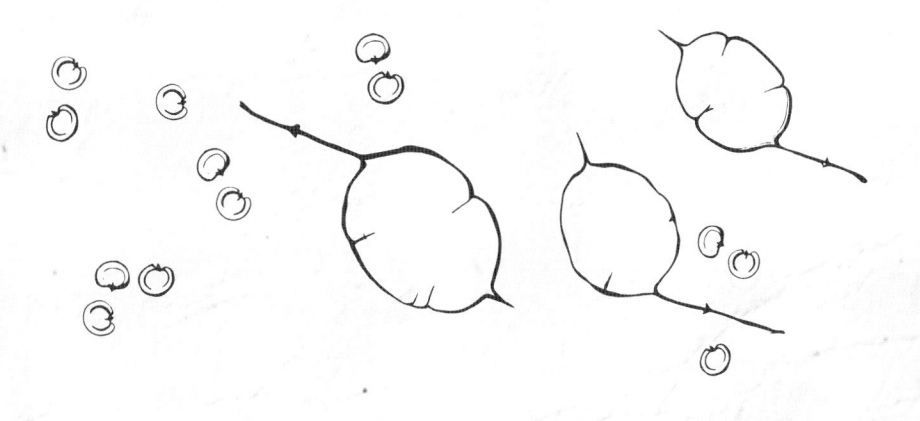

COLTSFOOT
Tussilago farfara

NAME ORIGIN:	*Tussis* is Latin for cough.
FAMILY:	Asteraceae

EDIBLE PART:	Flowers, roots and leaves
EDIBILITY RATING:	2
WHERE IT'S FOUND:	Damp ground, banks, roadsides, wasteland, meadow
CAUTIONS:	Contains saponins and pyrrolizidine alkaloids that can severely effect the liver in large quantities, but this enzyme is destroyed by heat, so made safe by cooking. Avoid if pregnant or breast-feeding.
LOOKALIKES:	*Petasites hybridus* – Butterbur. Coltsfoot has a largely scalloped leaf edge, white underside and yellow flowers on stalks, whereas Butterbur has no white underside to the leaves and pink multi-flowering stems.
MONTH SPAN:	Flowers February - April, the leaves tend to come after the flowers.

FOOD IDEAS:	The flowers can make a cordial, the root can be boiled and candied, the leaves can be eaten raw or cooked and washed to remove bitter parts. The burnt leaves can supposedly be used as a salt substitute.
OTHER INFO:	This is one of my favourite plants! At the age of 14, I did a couple of weeks work experience at Erddig, a National Trust garden in North Wales where I'd hang out with a Rastafarian called Derek, picking massive figs from the trees and munching them for our lunch. If you haven't been, I highly recommend it as it is a truly beautiful house and gardens, with an intriguing hydraulic ram called the cup and saucer. This was where I first saw coltsfoot when it was flowering and just starting to show its leaves. It was once used as a cough candy or syrup - it tastes pretty good but that might have been the quantity of sugar used!

HAVE A TRY

Chop a couple of handfuls of coltsfoot leaves and gently fry in a little butter for 5 minutes, then add a tablespoon or 2 of water to cover and simmer until soft. Toast some sesame seeds and sprinkle over to serve.

SWEET WOODRUFF
Galium odoratum

SYNONYM:	*Asperula odorata*
NAME ORIGIN:	*Galium* is derived from the word *gala* which means milk in Greek as it was used to flavour it and *odoratum* means scented (odour). The family Rubiaceae comes from *Rubia* meaning red as the roots produce a red dye.
FAMILY:	**Rubiaceae**
EDIBLE PART:	Flowers, leaves
EDIBILITY RATING:	3
WHERE IT'S FOUND:	Damp shade, semi shade, woodland, especially beech woodland, banks
CAUTIONS:	No known hazards but if you are drying it then dry it thoroughly with plenty of air circulation. The plant contains coumarins which give it the scent of new mown hay but if it is dried and gets damp in the process, then the coumarins change to dicoumarins which act as a strong anticoagulant causing internal bleeding.
LOOKALIKES:	The Bedstraw family all have whorls of leaves - cleavers *Galium aparine* is the one that sticks to fur or clothing, if the *Galium* has very fine leaves then it will be either Lady's bedstraw *Galium verum* which has small yellow flowers in clusters or hedge bedstraw *Galium mollugo* with little white flowers.
MONTH SPAN:	Flowers May - July, (Hz 5)

FOOD IDEAS:	The flowers can be eaten raw and the leaves raw or cooked. Try adding the leaves to fruit salads, make a tea from the fresh or dried aerial parts or use them to flavour milky puddings or drinks - it gives a sweet almond flavour. They can also be added to vodka, beer or jelly!

HOSTA
funkia
plantain lily

Hosta sp.

NAME ORIGIN:	**Named after the Austrian physician Nicolaus Thomas Host (1761 – 1834).**
FAMILY:	**Funkiaceae**
EDIBLE PART:	Leaves, shoots, stems
EDIBILITY RATING:	3
WHERE IT'S FOUND:	Shade, semi shade, gardens
MONTH SPAN:	Perennial, flowers July – September (Hz 4).

FOOD IDEAS:	Try the raw shoots (young leaves) eaten in salads or the cooked young leaves, shoots and stems. They work well in stir fries, soups and stews. Chop off any tough ends from the stalks. They need very little cooking so if you are adding them to a stir fry then 5 minutes is long enough to cook through.
OTHER INFO:	Not something you would think about eating! Depending on the species depends on the flavour as some are more tasty than others. Originates from Asia and has THE coolest family name! Hostas are seen as a vegetable in parts of Asia, especially in Japan. Make sure you only harvest a few shoots per plant so the plant can continue to grow well, and you get a second flush of tasty young shoots.

TULIP
WINE

(from Celtic wine making)
2 1/2 ltrs tulip petals
340ml white grape juice
concentrate
4 ltr water
900g sugar
2 tsp acid blend
50ml black tea
1 tsp yeast nutrient
1 packet white wine yeast

Put the petals in a fermenting bin. Boil the water and add the sugar and water to the bin, stirring until the sugar has dissolved. Cover and leave until luke warm. Add the rest of the ingredients, cover and keep in a warm place for 5 days.

Strain out the petals and pour into sterilized demi johns and seal with air locks. When the wine has finished fermenting (bubbling) then 'rack' into bottles (siphoning the liquid without disturbing the sediment) and cork. Leave for 6 months to a year.

TULIP

Tulipa sp.

NAME ORIGIN:	*Tulipa* is a corruption of the Persian word thoulyban or tulipant meaning turban from where the plant originates.
FAMILY:	Liliaceae

EDIBLE PART:	Flowers (and stems)
EDIBILITY RATING:	3
WHERE IT'S FOUND:	Cultivated gardens
CAUTIONS:	Avoid the bulbs as they contain tulipanin - an anthocyanin which gives plants their natural blue and purple hues, but tulipanin can cause severe dermatitis, especially in tulip pickers.
MONTH SPAN:	Flowers April - May.

FOOD IDEAS:	Use the petals to make wine, as a garnish or to serve creamy nibbles in like a tiny edible dish. Stuff the flowers (stem still attached) with all sorts - cooked couscous, cream cheese, cooked rice, greens and either steam for 3 minutes or dip in tempura batter and deep fry.
OTHER INFO:	Tulip-mania was a massive craze that started in the 1630s but unfortunately, the reason why tulips were starting to produce unusual colours and patterning was due to a type of mosaic virus called tulip break. The cross pollinating of these tulips to produce more and more varieties was weakening their structural make-up, making them susceptible to a disease called tulip fire which is pretty contagious with many bulb species. Notes on tulips say that bulbs can be cooked and eaten after leaching out toxins but I really would not risk it. In Holland during the war, the people would make flour from the bulbs by peeling and removing the centre of the bulb, drying it out completely then grinding into a powder to make bread - I heard it tasted pretty horrendous!

WATER BLINKS
Montia fontana

NAME ORIGIN:	**Water blinks have tiny white flowers which hardly open, hence the name.**
FAMILY:	**Portulacaceae**

EDIBLE PART:	Leaves
EDIBILITY RATING:	1
WHERE IT'S FOUND:	Pond-sides
LOOKALIKES:	*Stellaria uliginosa* bog stitchwort which is best not to eat in large quantities due to saponins. The differences are that bog stitchwort has straggly leaves and typical chickweed-like white flowers, whereas water blinks has fleshy leaves and white rounded small petals.
MONTH SPAN:	Flowers May - October, seeds ripen June - October

FOOD IDEAS:	Eat the leaves raw in salads.
OTHER INFO:	This is a very global plant which grows anywhere from the tropics to the arctic.

MUGWORT
Artemisia vulgaris

SYNONYM:	*Absinthium spicatum, Artemisia affinis, Artemisia coarctata, Artemisia officinalis*
NAME ORIGIN:	The plant is named after Artemis the Greek goddess (also known as Diana) and the term *vulgaris* means common. The name mugwort possibly comes from the Norse word muggi meaning marsh as to where it can be found growing.
FAMILY:	Asteraceae

EDIBLE PART:	Young leaves, stems and flower heads
EDIBILITY RATING:	2
WHERE IT'S FOUND:	Waysides, roadsides, hedgerows, marshland
LOOKALIKES:	Similar looking to other artemisias and to feverfew *Tanacetum parthenium* except mugwort has green leaves with a whitish underside and dense dark red flowerhead clusters, whereas feverfew has green leaves on the top and underside, and small daisy-like flowers.
CAUTIONS:	Contains thujone in small quantities so don't consume too much, avoid if pregnant and it can induce abortion. Also avoid if you are allergic to hazelnuts!
MONTH SPAN:	Perennial (Hz 3) flowers July - September.

FOOD IDEAS:	Mugwort used to flavour beer and ale due to its bitter flavours, the dried leaves can be used as a tea and as a food flavouring - its bitterness stimulates appetite. It is added to soups, rice dishes and many other savoury meals.
OTHER INFO:	Mugwort has been smoked, made into tea or put under pillows to enhance dreams but not to be taken over a long period of time due to the toxic build up of thujone.

COWSLIP
Primula veris

SYNONYM:	*Primula officinalis*
NAME ORIGIN:	*Primus* is Latin for the first as it is early flowering and *veris* means springtime.
FAMILY:	Primulaceae

EDIBLE PART:	Leaves, flowers
EDIBILITY RATING:	2
WHERE IT'S FOUND:	Fields, meadows, grassland
LOOKALIKES:	Primrose *Primula vulgaris* leaves look similar but primrose flowers are flat, open and each on a single stem, whereas cowslip flowers are in clusters on one stem, they are much smaller and hang down. Oxslip *Primula elatior* looks very similar but with larger pale clusters of flowers that look more like primrose flowers.
CAUTIONS:	Some people are allergic to the stamens. The plant contains saponins so eat in small quantities, avoid if you have high blood pressure and it can cause gastrointestinal upsets. Avoid if pregnant.
MONTH SPAN:	(Hz 5) Flowers April - May.

FOOD IDEAS:	Eat the leaves raw or cooked, use it as a good winter salad filler, the flowers can be used as a garnish and were once used for a tonic wine. Cowslip pudding was once a common dessert to make, with plenty of sugar and plenty of cream! The leaves are a little bitter but the flowers do taste like sunshine and are relatively sweet.
OTHER INFO:	Due to changes in farming practices a few decades ago, cowslip population declined dramatically so is classed as rare, even though if when you find it, it is abundant. Pick sparingly and don't uproot.

LADY'S SMOCK DIP

1 cup cream cheese
1/2 a lemon plus zest
1 tbsp finely chopped lady's smock (leaves, stem, flowers plus some for garnish)
seasoning

In a bowl mix the cream cheese, lemon juice, zest and lady's smock together until combined well. Taste and season accordingly. Serve with vegetable crudités or thin crackers (or both, go on, push the boat out!).

LADY'S SMOCK

cuckoo flower, milk maids

Cardamine pratensis

NAME ORIGIN:	*Kardia* means heart and *damao* means to subdue, as it was once used as a heart sedative. *Pratensis* is Latin for meadow.
FAMILY:	**Brassicaceae**
EDIBLE PART:	Flowers, leaves
EDIBILITY RATING:	3
WHERE IT'S FOUND:	Bog gardens, streams, semi to full shade
LOOKALIKES:	Leaves look very similar when young to hairy bittercress *Cardamine hirsuta* – both are edible and of the same genus.
MONTH SPAN:	Flowers April to June

FOOD IDEAS:	It grows in the graveyard at St Enoder! Jo spotted its delicate pink flowers growing amongst the three cornered leek. It is the perfect garnish for a nettle roulade or good for a slight bite in a salad. Eat the flowers and leaves for a mild peppery flavour.
OTHER INFO:	Lady's smock is rich in vitamin C and is an excellent appetite stimulant. The plant is supposedly sacred to fairies.

"AND LADY-SMOCKS ALL SILVER-WHITE, AND CUCKOO-BUDS OF YELLOW HUE, DO PAINT THE MEADOWS WITH DELIGHT."

Love's Labour's Lost, act V, scene 2, Shakespeare

FERNS

Matteuccia struthiopteris shuttlecock fern, ostrich fern
Osmunda regalis royal fern

NAME ORIGIN:	*Struthio* comes from the Ancient Greek for ostrich and the word *pteris* means wing as the branching fronds resemble wings.
	The name *Osmunda* possibly derives from the Saxon word for strength as it is a tall and robust fern, or from Osmunder which is one of the names for Scandinavian Thor. *Regalis* means regal or royal.
FAMILY:	Onocleaceae; Osmundaceae
EDIBLE PART:	Fiddleheads also known as croziers
EDIBILITY RATING:	2
WHERE IT'S FOUND:	Shade, woodland, damp areas, river banks; Woodland, fens, damp ground
CAUTIONS:	Many ferns contain carcinogens and thiaminase, which can deplete the body of vitamin B complex, but cooking kills off this enzyme and a good healthy diet helps prevent any adverse effect.
LOOKALIKES:	It can be hard to identify one fern species from another. Viewed from above, *Matteuccia* looks like a shuttlecock facing towards the ground, with soft feathery fern fronds. Royal fern *Osmunda* is quite an easy one to identify with smooth stems and smooth solid fronds (not at all feathery in appearance).
MONTH SPAN:	(Hz 2) Croziers appear from April for both ferns.
FOOD IDEAS:	Flake off any scaly parts of the shuttlecock croziers. Boil the croziers for 10 minutes as with all edible ferns, chuck the water and repeat to leech out the toxins. Eat it as it is after this process or use it as a vegetable. Try adding to omelettes with cheddar or goat's cheese.

OTHER INFO: *Matteuccia* is the best tasting fern in my opinion. Did you know that a newly identified genus of fern has been named after Lady Gaga?! This new genus includes names such as *Gaga germanotta* after her real name Stefani Germanotta and *Gaga monstraparva*, meaning little monster (like her fan base). This plant reproduces with spores that grow to be male, female or both... When harvesting, pick with your thumbnail and finger, leaving at least 3 croziers remaining on the plant.

BIBIMBAP

cooked rice
fern croziers
bean sprouts
spinach
cucumber
courgette
carrot
(beef optional)
eggs
Korean red pepper paste
sesame oil
sea salt or soya sauce

Bibimbap is a Korean recipe which is made up of cooked rice as a base, then a selection of vegetables, including fern croziers, bean sprouts, spinach, cucumber, courgette, carrot and beef as an optional extra, topped with a fried egg sunny-side up and a dressing of Korean red pepper paste and sesame oil. There are many variations of this but the cucumber is salted to draw out the water, the spinach and bean sprouts are steamed, the fern croziers are cooked as mentioned (boiled twice with water changes) and the remaining ingredients are sautéed, all served with either just a little sea salt or with sesame oil and a little soya sauce. All the vegetables are added to the rice separately, topped with the egg then the dressing drizzled over it.

HEDGE BEDSTRAW

Galium mollugo

SYNONYM:	*Galium elatum, Galium erectum*
NAME ORIGIN:	The word *gala* is Greek for milk; *Galium verum* was once used for flavouring milk.
FAMILY:	Rubiaceae
EDIBLE PART:	Leaves
EDIBILITY RATING:	2
WHERE IT'S FOUND:	Open ground, hedgerow, dappled shade, grassland
LOOKALIKES:	Most galiums look alike but this one looks especially like a skinny version of sweet woodruff with little white flowers.
CAUTIONS:	No, but the plant contains coumarins which give the scent of new mown hay and if you dry it in a damp environment, it can convert to dicoumarins which act as an anticoagulant and can cause internal bleeding.
MONTH SPAN:	Flowers June - September.

FOOD IDEAS:	Eat the leaves raw or cooked.

ST GEORGE'S MUSHROOM

Calocybe gambosa

SYNONYM:	*Tricholoma gambosum, Tricholoma georgii, Lyophyllum gambosum*
NAME ORIGIN:	In Italy it is known as marzolino as it appears in March and in Germany maipilz as it appears in May. *Calocybe* comes from the Ancient Greek *kalos* meaning pretty, and *cubos* meaning head.
FAMILY:	Lycophyllaceae

EDIBLE PART:	Mushroom
EDIBILITY RATING:	3
WHERE IT'S FOUND:	Grassy areas, lawns, pastures, often forming rings
LOOKALIKES:	Deadly fibrecap *Inocybe erubescens* looks most similar, but it grows in woodlands and appears at the end of May in the UK (nor does it smell mealy or cucumber-like, like St George's mushroom). The *Inocybe* also bruises red, where St George's mushroom doesn't.
CAUTIONS:	None known.
MONTH SPAN:	Spring (late April but varies due to changing climate).

FOOD IDEAS:	Slice and fry in butter, grill, pickle.
OTHER INFO:	Today is St. George's Day. St George was born in Turkey to Christian parents. He joined the Roman army in Palestine and when the Emperor Diocletian was wiping out Christians, he resigned his military post and even though tortured, George remained true to his faith. According to Medieval legend, the town of Selene in Libya had a dragon nesting by their fresh water spring so they couldn't fetch water without a sacrifice of a sheep each time. They eventually ran out of sheep so they had to sacrifice themselves and the first was to be the Monarch's daughter Cleolinda. Fortunately (although not for the dragon) St George happened to be riding past, he slayed the dragon and rescued Cleolinda.

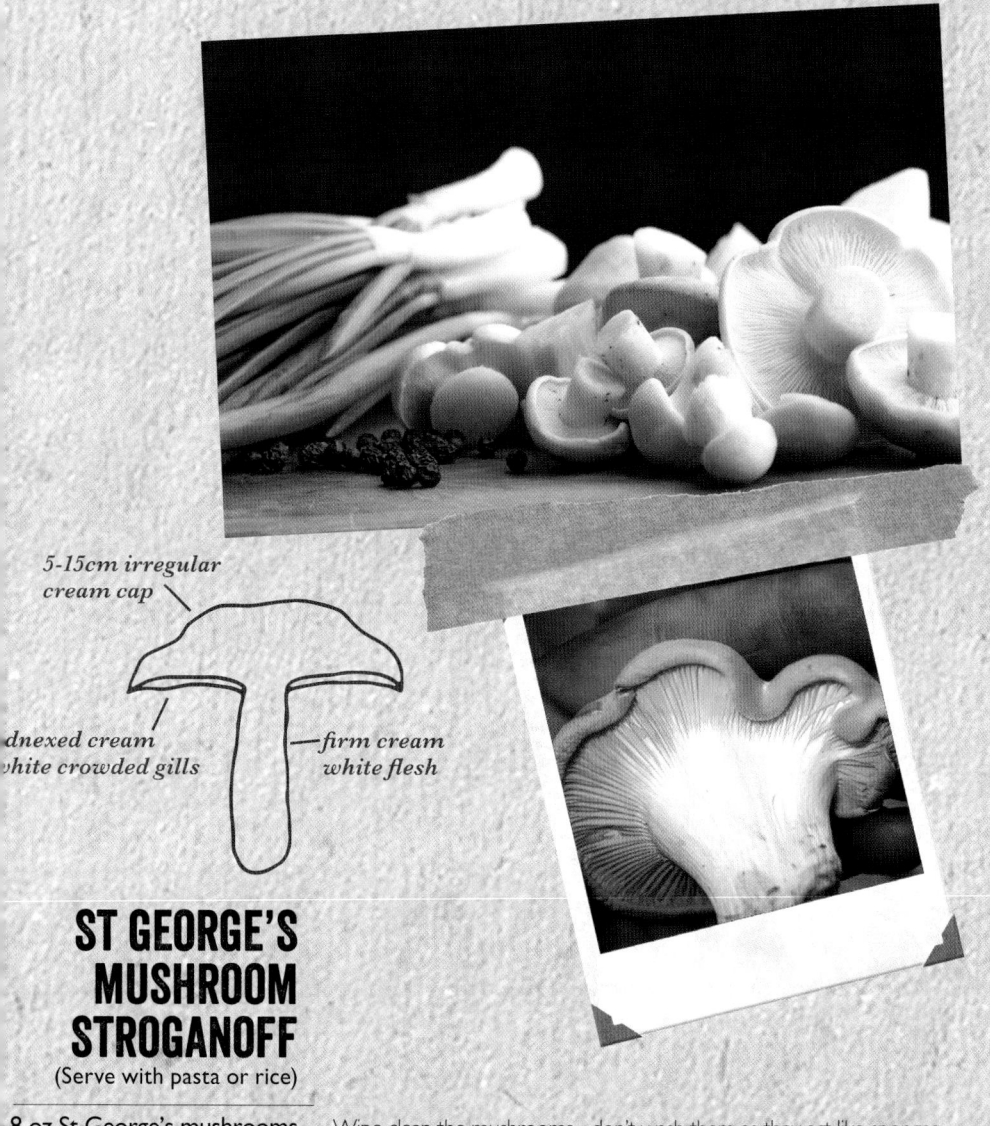

5-15cm irregular
cream cap

*unnexed cream
white crowded gills*

*firm cream
white flesh*

ST GEORGE'S MUSHROOM STROGANOFF

(Serve with pasta or rice)

-8 oz St George's mushrooms cleaned and finely sliced
50g butter
1 clove of garlic (or 5 ramson leaves, washed and shredded)
1/2 tsp paprika
double cream
sea salt and black pepper

Wipe clean the mushrooms - don't wash them as they act like sponges and soak up the water. Get the pasta or rice on the boil, then start the rest of the cooking. Slice up the mushrooms and fry in a saucepan with the butter, garlic and paprika, turning the mushroom slices until getting a little colour. They exude a fair bit of water when they cook so you may need to pour this away. Add the cream and simmer to thicken. Season and serve on the rice or pasta.

SOLOMON'S SEAL
Polygonatum multiflorum

SYNONYM:	*Convallaria ambigua, Convallaria broteroi, Convallaria bracteata, Polygonatum salamonis*
NAME ORIGIN:	*Multiflorum* means many flowers, *polygonum* comes from the Greek *polys* meaning many and *gonu* means joints (referring to the knotted roots).
FAMILY:	Asparagaceae (Convallariaceae)

EDIBLE PART:	Young shoots, cooked (roots can be cooked)
EDIBILITY RATING:	2
WHERE IT'S FOUND:	Woodland
CAUTIONS:	Related to Lily of the Valley *Convallaria* which is a very powerful heart medicine that can be fatal. The berries can be very poisonous in large quantities. Avoid if pregnant or breast feeding.
MONTH SPAN:	(Hz 4) Perennial, flowers June

FOOD IDEAS:	Steam or briefly boil the young shoots and eat like asparagus. Pick them before the leaves start to unfurl. The roots need leaching to remove bitterness and then cooked. Great in dishes like quiches or pasta, or by themselves.
OTHER INFO:	Solomon's seal is quite a remarkable plant, and is used in Chinese medicine for anti-ageing, preventing heart disease and promoting fertility. Known as Fo-ti, it is a bit of an all-rounder reducing cholesterol, treating menopausal symptoms, tuberculosis, protecting skin from harmful UV rays... the list is endless!

MOREL
Morchella esculenta

NAME ORIGIN:	The word *esculenta* derives from the Latin meaning edible.
FAMILY:	Morchellaceae

EDIBLE PART:	Mushroom
EDIBILITY RATING:	4
WHERE IT'S FOUND:	Gardens, woodland, waste ground
CAUTION:	All morels need to be cooked as otherwise they cause stomach upsets.
LOOKALIKES:	Pouched false morel - poisonous *Gyromitra infula*, false morel *Gyromitra esculenta* - can cause stomach upsets and a build up of toxins. There are lots of other similar looking species that are poisonous or can cause stomach upsets but the main difference is that morels have a honeycomb structure where false morels have a convoluted or brain-like structure.
MONTH SPAN:	Late March - May

FOOD IDEAS:	Mushroom linguini, wild mushroom risotto, morel bruschetta.
OTHER INFO:	Can be found in bark mulch which acts as a camouflage for these crafty little fellas!

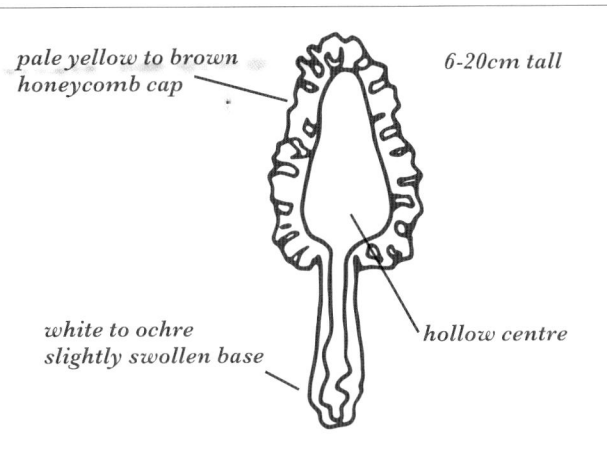

pale yellow to brown
honeycomb cap

6-20cm tall

white to ochre
slightly swollen base

hollow centre

lookalike *Gyromitra esculenta* false morel

MOREL
BRUSCHETTA

1 tbsp olive oil	Shake the morels and check for insects. You can leave them to soak in
1 tbsp butter	briny water, but mushrooms act like sponges so I prefer not to do this.
6 or more morels	Chop into 1cm pieces. Slice the baguette at an angle and toast. Heat
crème fraiche or cream	the oil and butter in a pan until fairly hot, add the mushrooms, tossing
1 baguette	to coat and when golden, add the thyme. When the toast is ready,
1 garlic clove	rub with a garlic clove. Just before taking the morels off the heat, add a
thyme	small dollop of creme fraiche and warm through gently. Serve on the
seasoning	bruschetta and season to taste.

BULRUSH reedmace, cattail
Typha latifolia

NAME ORIGIN:	*Latifolia* comes from the Latin word meaning broad leaf, the genus *Typha* comes from the Greek 'tufh' or 'typhe' which means bulrush, cattail.
FAMILY:	**Typhaceae**
EDIBLE PART:	Rhizomes, shoots, seed/pollen, young stems
EDIBILITY RATING:	4
WHERE IT'S FOUND:	Shallow water, streams, ditches, ponds
CAUTIONS:	No known hazards except emmenagogue.
LOOKALIKES:	Don't get it muddled with *Iris* sp. as some can be poisonous. The seed heads both old and new are a good indicator.
MONTH SPAN:	Flowers June – August, Hz 3.
OTHER DATES:	For roots see December 13th.

FOOD IDEAS:	Eat the stem raw or cooked and the rhizomes and shoots (white parts). The roasted seed can be eaten or ground into a flour and cooked with and the pollen can be eaten raw or cooked. The only reason you can't eat every part is because the green parts are too fibrous to eat. Roast, thinly slice and eat raw, boil, fry - it's all delicious! Tastes quite like corn (and popcorn!). Use the dried ground flour (from the seeds or even the rhizomes) as a wheat flour additive to add flavour and richness.
OTHER INFO:	Collect from a clean source.

SWINE WARTCRESS
Coronopus didymus

SYNONYM:	*Lepidium didymum, Senebiera didyma*
NAME ORIGIN:	*Corvus* means crow (my husband has a Gibson Corvus guitar, which looks like a crow in flight). The Greek word *podos* or *pous* means foot.
FAMILY:	Brassicaceae

EDIBLE PART:	Leaves
EDIBILITY RATING:	2
WHERE IT'S FOUND:	Cultivated fields, waste ground
MONTH SPAN:	Flowers June - September, seeds ripen August - October

FOOD IDEAS:	The leaves of swinecress have a peppery bite to them so they can be a good addition to salads. Crowfoot needs boiling first as it has a strong unpleasant flavour when raw.

SWINECRESS crowfoot
Coronopus squamatus

SYNONYM:	*Cochlearia coronopus, Senebiera coronopus, Coronopus ruellii, Coronopus procumbens*
WHERE IT'S FOUND:	Coastal, sandy, well walked paths

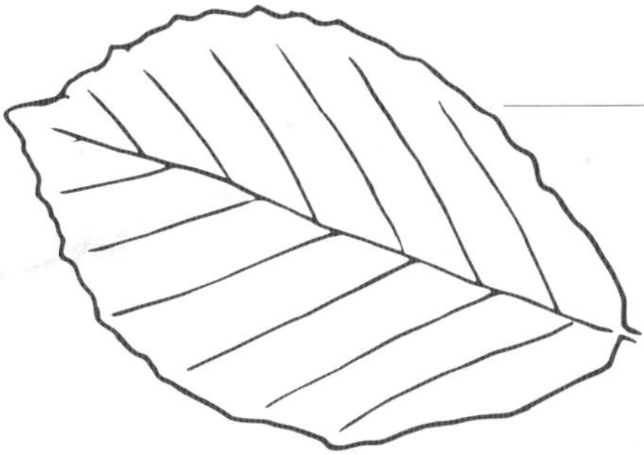

BEECH
LEAF NOYAU

Adapted from the Roger
Phillips recipe - this is what I
remember of it anyway!

1/2 carrier bag of fresh young
beech leaves
1 bottle of gin
1 glass of brandy
sugar to taste
a large glass sweet jar with a lid
or something similar

Wash the leaves and pack them into the jar, pouring the bottle of gin on to them, pushing the leaves under the liquid. Put the lid on and leave for 2-3 weeks, shaking occasionally. Strain keeping the liquid(!), squeezing the leaves well to get every drop, then add the glass of brandy and sugar to taste - this is a liqueur so it will be fairly sweet. I think it tastes quite like Benedictine.

BEECH
Fagus sylvatica

NAME ORIGIN:	*Fagus* is the Latin for beech, *sylvatica* refers to growing in woods.
FAMILY:	**Fagaceae**

EDIBLE PART:	Young leaves
EDIBILITY RATING:	3
WHERE IT'S FOUND:	Woodlands or grown as hedges
CAUTIONS:	Only seeds appear to be toxic in large quantities and the residue from the seeds can be an irritant.
MONTH SPAN:	Quite late to come into leaf, flowers from April - May.
OTHER DATES:	Seeds ripen September - October. For seeds, see November 6th.

FOOD IDEAS:	Beech leaf noyau is seriously good - I know it is in most foraging cookbooks but you really must try it! The young leaves are palatable and a good addition to salads.
OTHER INFO:	Beech is a tree sacred to the Celts and was used to gain insight into the future from ancient knowledge and as a symbol of prosperity. In the Victorians' 'language of flowers', beech means 'prosperity'. Thin slices of beech wood were once used to write on and the words beech and book come from the Anglo-Saxon word boc. Writing was seen as a powerful way of making magic into reality and it is believed that if you write a wish on a piece of beech wood and bury it, it will come true.

SEA TROUT (Called Sewin in Wales)

Salmo trutta (sometimes subspecies trutta)

NAME ORIGIN:	The word *trutta* is Latin for trout.
FAMILY:	Salmonidae
EDIBLE PART:	Meat
EDIBILITY RATING:	5
WHERE IT'S FOUND:	Sea
CAUTIONS:	Avoid if you have fish allergies.
MONTH SPAN:	16th April - 30th September.

FOOD IDEAS:	Fantastically substantial fish that can be grilled, stuffed, pan fried, en papillote, roasted, smoked and goes well with watercress, beetroot and lemon sauces such as a lemony hollandaise.
OTHER INFO:	Sea trout is very similar to salmon. Brown trout and sea trout are practically the same fish, except one lot has decided to move from the fresh water rivers to the sea! They don't venture much further than a 5 mile radius out to sea. Slob trout are trout that venture part way in to estuaries but never go out to sea - lazy!
	To catch sea trout, try a 10ft floating line at night. Take a torch but don't shine it on the water and a net for landing the fish. Sea trout flies vary in size and colour.

STUFFED SEA TROUT
(serves 4)

4 gutted and cleaned trout
1 tbsp butter
12-15 button or small field mushrooms
1 clove of garlic
4 tbsp toasted flaked almonds
1 bunch of chervil
1 handful of lemon thyme
seasoning
cocktail sticks

Wipe and slice the mushrooms. In a frying pan, melt the butter and fry the mushrooms until golden. Finely chop the garlic and add this to the pan, frying for 1 minute. Roughly chop the herbs and in a bowl, mix all the remaining ingredients together (apart from the fish and cocktail sticks!). Open up each fish and stuff the mixture in and 'sew up' with the cocktail sticks to prevent the filling falling out. Pan fry the sea trout on a low heat to cook all the way through, turning to cook well on both sides. Serve with salad or vegetables, rice or potatoes.

LEMON BALM CUPCAKES
(makes 12)

Preheat the oven to 180 degrees C. Cream the butter and sugar together until pale and fluffy. Mix in the lemon balm. Beat the eggs and add them in and mix thoroughly. Add the flour and fold in carefully, then spoon into paper cases and bake in the oven for 10-16 minutes, checking to get the perfect golden colouring. Delicate lemony flavour, which you can enhance with a lemon balm infused cream cheese icing.

110g caster sugar
110g butter
3-4 tbsp finely chopped lemon balm
2 eggs
110g self raising flour

LEMON BALM
Heidi balm

Melissa officinalis

SYNONYM:	*Thymus melissa, Mutelia officinalis, Faucibarba officinalis*
NAME ORIGIN:	*Mel* means honey; *melissa* is Greek for bee, *Melisophyllon* is Greek for 'beloved by bees'. *Officinalis* means of the apothecary's shop as it is medicinal.
FAMILY:	**Lamiaceae**

EDIBLE PART:	Leaves
EDIBILITY RATING:	4
WHERE IT'S FOUND:	Gardens, garden escapee, waste ground
CAUTIONS:	Emmenagogue so avoid during pregnancy, can cause irritation with sensitive skin.
LOOKALIKES:	Lemon balm looks like many plants in the mint family, but by crushing or tearing the leaves, you'll get the lemony hit.
MONTH SPAN:	Flowers June - October (Hz 4).

FOOD IDEAS:	Eat the leaves raw or cooked as they impart a delicious lemony flavour. Can be added to alcoholic drinks such as Pimms, eaten in salads, cooked as a stuffing for meat or sauces, sweet or savoury, or make a tea.
OTHER INFO:	A very invasive plant from my childhood! We moved from Canada to England when I was less than 3 years old and moved in to a hotel for a few months. Percy was the gardener who helped moved my plastic green box of toys to our room in the eaves. In the gardens of the hotel, Percy grew many plants which I guess were used in the hotel. This was my first experience of plants being grown and I was fascinated by carrots growing and Heidi balm which smelled strongly of lemons - in the background was the smell of 2 stroke engine oil from the boats on the river, one of my favourite smells! The plant is uplifting and calming - great as a herbal tea.

crab & lobster

sea lettuce

bass

swinecress

sea beet

MAY

sea beet

hree cornered leek

hoary cress

YHA

JAPANESE KNOTWEED
Fallopia japonica

SYNONYM:	*Polygonum cuspidatum, Reynoutria japonica*
NAME ORIGIN:	*Japonica* means Japanese, unsure of the origin of the genus.
FAMILY:	Polygonaceae

EDIBLE PART:	New shoots - see cautions
EDIBILITY RATING:	5
WHERE IT'S FOUND:	Dappled shade, hedge. It has naturalised throughout the countryside.
CAUTIONS:	Contains oxalic acid (as does rhubarb and sorrel) so may aggravate rheumatism, arthritis and kidney stones. Be careful where you harvest this from as it is an invasive plant and is often sprayed with chemicals to eradicate it.
MONTH SPAN:	Shoots from March, flowers July - October, seeds ripen August - October.

FOOD IDEAS:	Think of it as rhubarb and cook it the same way, stewed, baked in pies, etc.

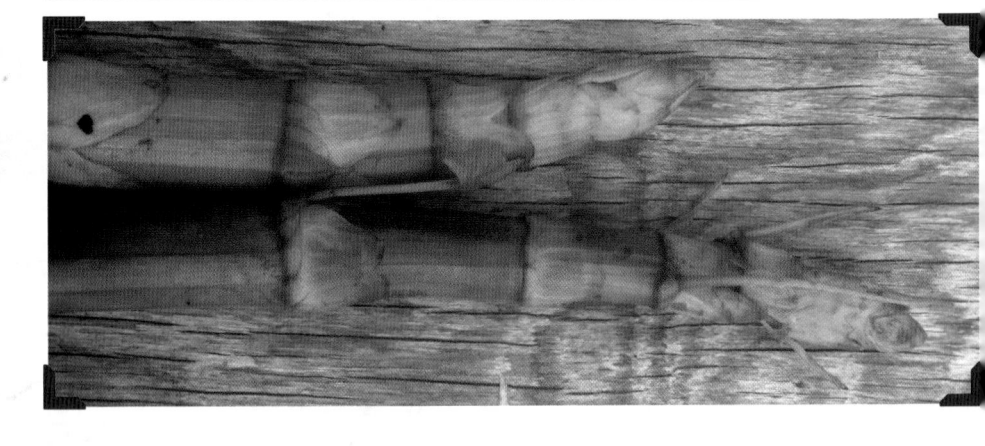

KNOTWEED JAM

175g knotweed shoots
150g jam sugar
1 tbsp ginger beer

If you find a patch that you know hasn't been sprayed to kill it off, then you are in for a treat and even better, you'll be doing your conservational bit for eradicating and controlling the extremely invasive knotweed! You may need to take the mountain to Mohammed so grab yourself a little camping cooker, saucepan, a bag of jam sugar, scales, and a bottle of ginger beer. The reason behind this, as well as the delights of cooking alfresco is that knotweed is such an invasive species, therefore it is an offence to take it from its original site in case you spread it (intentionally or otherwise) and you will be breaking the law!

So… pick the young tender shoots that are appearing out of the ground like stunning cerise-pink asparagus. Pick as much as you can. If you give a gentle flex to the knotweed shoots, you can make the executive decision whether you need to peel the base or not as the outer skin can become tough as the plant grows.

Weigh the shoots once chopped and weigh a little less jam sugar than the weight of the shoots e.g. 175g shoots to 150g sugar.

Put the shoots, sugar and a tbsp of ginger beer into the saucepan and heat gently until the jam wrinkles when pushed gently on a cold spoon (you'd normally put a plate in the fridge and test the jam by dropping it onto the plate and pushing it with your finger - when it wrinkles, it is ready). Put it into a sterile jar and seal it. The jam doesn't take long to do at all and feel free to vary it with other flavours. Try knotweed jam and scones with cream (jam first - Cornish style), knotweed cream and elderflower jelly or knotweed meringue pie!

HEDGE BINDWEED
Calystegia sepium

SYNONYM:	*Convolvulus sepium*
NAME ORIGIN:	*Calyx* is Greek for cup and *stege* means a covering referring to the calyx enclosed in 2 bracts. *Sepium* means of hedges.
FAMILY:	**Convolvulaceae**
EDIBLE PART:	Roots, stems
EDIBILITY RATING:	2
WHERE IT'S FOUND:	In your garden where you don't want it, hedgerows
LOOKALIKES:	Sea bindweed (*Calystegia soldanella*) which grows in dunes and any coastal region. The main differences are the small pink flowers and the small scurvygrass-like leaves, compared to the large white flowers and large floppy square-heart shaped leaves. Sea bindweed also has edible shoots when cooked or pickled but also can act as a purgative.
CAUTIONS:	Yes – take in small amounts as it can act as a purgative.
MONTH SPAN:	Flowers June - September (Hz 4)

FOOD IDEAS:	I'm so pleased you can eat this!!! Finally revenge!!! I have this all over the garden and I have now overcome my hatred for it, now I know I can get my own back. Simmer or boil it in water until tender and eat.

WILD CABBAGE
Brassica oleracea

SYNONYM:	*Brassica sylvestris*
NAME ORIGIN:	*Bresic* is Celtic for cabbage, *oleracea* means edible or cultivated. The word cabbage comes from the Latin *caput* meaning head.
FAMILY:	Brassicaceae

EDIBLE PART:	Leaves (leave the seeds)
EDIBILITY RATING:	4
WHERE IT'S FOUND:	Cliffs, coastal
MONTH SPAN:	Flowers May - August, seeds ripen July - September, (Hz 7). Can be harvested all year round, as long as it isn't a hard winter.

FOOD IDEAS:	Eat the leaves raw or cooked. The raw leaves have a slight warmth to them and I shred them and mix them with grated carrot, mayo and salad cream to make coleslaw. Shredded leaves can be deep fried and sprinkled with sesame seeds, sea salt and a pinch of sugar to make a Chinese style fake crispy seaweed (crispy seaweed in the UK IS made from shredded cabbage!). Simply steamed and served with butter it is delicious. Bubble and squeak! Wild cabbage also goes well with juniper berries.
OTHER INFO:	This plant is pretty rare but it does grow near where my Mum and Dad live! Today, Dad and I did the Rotary Club 4 1/2 mile ramble along the coastal path and guess what?! I found it!! In the back of my mind, I remember seeing it when I was quite young, but haven't seen it since. As it is really rare, I can't tell you the exact location, but if you do find it, then harvest sensibly by only taking 2-4 fresh leaves from a plant depending on the size, and always leave the centre, the seeds plus plenty of leaves to carry on growing and photosynthesizing.

STUFFED CABBAGE ROLLS

8-10 large wild cabbage leaves
1/3 cup pearl barley cooked and drained
1 large red onion
1 lb minced pork, lamb or beef
1 egg
1 can of tinned tomatoes
1 stock cube
thyme
seasoning

Parboil the cabbage leaves for about 5 minutes. If the midribs on the leaves are too thick and make it too difficult to roll, then remove them. Peel and finely dice the onion and fry until soft. In a bowl, mix together the onion, minced meat, egg, seasoning and thyme. Lay out a cabbage leaf and put a spoonful of the mixture at the base so you can pull the sides in and roll up in to a small 'spring roll' like shape. Use a cocktail stick to hold it together. Do the same for the rest of the cabbage leaves and meat mixture. In a bowl or food processor, empty the tin of tomatoes and blitz or mash until smooth. Put the cabbage rolls in a saucepan, pour over the tomato liquid and stock cube. Cover and simmer for about an hour - you may need to top up with a little water so keep an eye on it. Serve in a bowl with crusty bread.

ASPARAGUS AND GOAT'S CHEESE TART

Preheat oven to 190 degrees C. Either by hand or in a food processor mix the flour and butter together, adding the water last to combine. Roll out to line a quiche or flan dish, prick with a fork and line with baking parchment and dried beans to bake blind for about 10 minutes until the pastry is cooked but not showing colour. Snip the base ends off the asparagus where they are tough and steam the asparagus for about 5 minutes.

Drain and cut into 2-3 inch (5cm) lengths and spread about the pastry case, then dice the goat's cheese and do the same. With a balloon whisk mix the eggs, cream, chives and seasoning and pour over the asparagus and goats cheese, then pop in the oven for about half an hour until baked and golden on top. Eat hot or cold.

For the pastry
6 oz plain flour
4 oz butter
2 tbsp cold water

For the filling
15-20 asparagus
130g pack of goat's cheese
4 eggs
150ml single cream
a good handful of crow garlic stems or chives
seasoning

ASPARAGUS

wild asparagus

Asparagus officinalis

NAME ORIGIN:	The Greek word *sparasso* means to tear due to its thorny parts and *officinalis* always shows a plant was used medicinally.
FAMILY:	Asparagaceae

EDIBLE PART:	Young shoots
EDIBILITY RATING:	5
WHERE IT'S FOUND:	Sandy fertile soil
CAUTIONS:	Asparagus can irritate kidneys if consumed in quantity, the berries are a little poisonous. Wild asparagus is slightly bitter and thinner in comparison to cultivated asparagus.
MONTH SPAN:	April - June

FOOD IDEAS:	Delicious steamed and griddled, served with homemade hollandaise or just a good squeeze of lemon juice and black pepper. Use in soups, tarts, stir fries.
OTHER INFO:	Eating asparagus makes your wee smell. Medicinally asparagus helps to improve the digestive system, is an anti-inflammatory and an antioxidant, both of which help with heart disease and type 2 diabetes. It is also linked with leukaemia treatments.

PEDUNCULATE OAK
Quercus robur

SYNONYM	*Quercus pedunculata*
NAME ORIGIN:	***Quercus*** **is the Latin name for oak tree. In Celtic the word** ***quer*** **means fine, and** ***cuez*** **means tree.**
FAMILY:	**Fagaceae**
EDIBLE PART:	Young leaves (for acorns, see Oct 30th)
EDIBILITY RATING:	2
WHERE IT'S FOUND:	Deciduous woodland
CAUTIONS:	Oak can cause possible digestive problems. It can be difficult to digest and can delay absorption of alkaline drugs.
MONTH SPAN:	In leaf from May

FOOD IDEAS:	Infuse to make flavoured liqueurs or make oak leaf wine.
OTHER INFO:	Oak galls produce a black ink and hair dye.

OAK
LEAF WINE

Wash the leaves and pick through for pests and damaged leaves. Put the leaves in a brewing bucket, cover with boiling water and leave overnight. Strain and keep the liquid, discarding the leaves. Put the liquid in a large saucepan or 2 if you don't have one big enough and add the sugar, juice and zest of the lemon and oranges equally between pans.

(from Farmers Weekly 1970)
1 gallon of oak leaves
1 lemon
4 oranges
4lb sugar
wine yeast

Bring to the boil and reduce the heat, simmering for 20 minutes. When cool pour the liquid through a muslin cloth into a demi-john. Put the yeast in a glass and add a little hand-hot water (not boiling) to activate it and add to the demi-john, then top it up with cooled boiled water until almost full. Add the bung with air lock. Leave it to ferment and when the air lock has stopped bubbling, rack the liquid into wine bottles and leave for 6 months. The longer it is left, the better it gets.

BEER BATTERED SCAMPI WITH TARTARE SAUCE

Sunflower oil to deep fry
30 langoustine tails peeled
and deveined
plain flour for dusting

For the batter
8oz self raising flour
pinch of bicarbonate of soda
pinch of sea salt
8 fl.oz ice cold lager

Tartare sauce
3 tbsp mayonnaise
6 gherkins finely chopped
1/2 shallot finely chopped
1 tbsp capers finely chopped
1 tbsp parsley finely chopped
1 tbsp dill finely chopped
1/2 lemon
sea salt and black pepper

To make the tartare sauce, combine all the ingredients in a bowl, squeezing the lemon into a cupped hand to stop the pips falling in. In a separate bowl, put the self raising flour, bicarb of soda and sea salt. Using a balloon whisk to beat together add the beer slowly and beat hard to prevent lumps.

Heat the oil in a saucepan - if you drop a small cube of bread in it and it rises to the surface and goes golden quickly, then the oil is ready. While the oil is heating, take the langoustine tails and dust them in the plain flour (this helps the batter stick to them). Dip the langoustines into the batter and deep fry until golden. Remove with a slotted spoon and drain on kitchen roll. Serve with chips, salad or both and don't forget a quarter of lemon to squeeze over.

DUBLIN BAY PRAWN

Dublin Bay prawn
langoustine
Norway lobster
scampi!

Nephrops norvegicus

NAME ORIGIN:	*Norvegicus* means Norwegian, hence the name Norway lobster. Their eyes are kidney shaped, hence the Ancient Greek *nephros* meaning kidney and *ops*, eye.
FAMILY:	Nephropidae

EDIBLE PART:	Meat
EDIBILITY RATING:	5
WHERE IT'S FOUND:	Muddy seabed
CAUTIONS:	Avoid if you have shellfish allergies
MONTH SPAN:	September - May

FOOD IDEAS:	Barbecue, grill, boil. Don't forget to take out the poo-pipe! This can get pretty messy!!
OTHER INFO:	Did you know that scampi is not an actual animal (Nick?!) but is actually langoustine tails?

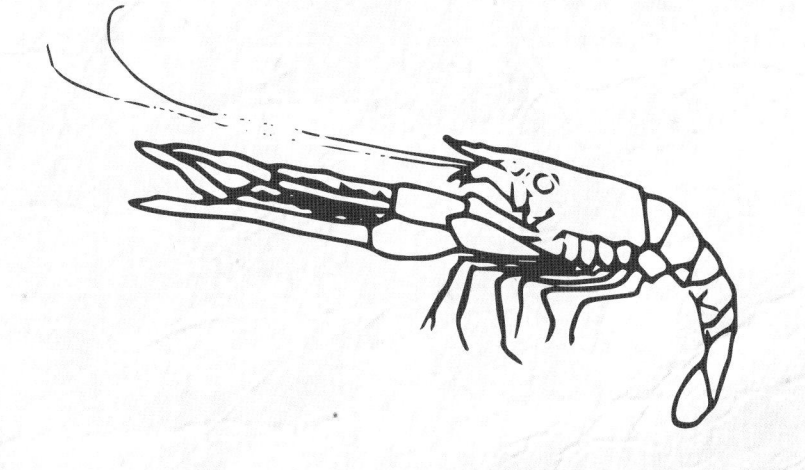

CAT'S EAR
Hypochoeris radicata

NAME ORIGIN:	*Hypo* is Greek for under, *chaeris* (*choeris*) is beauty and *radicata* means circular.
FAMILY:	**Asteraceae**

EDIBLE PART:	Leaves
EDIBILITY RATING:	2
WHERE IT'S FOUND:	Lawns, meadows, waste ground
LOOKALIKES:	Dandelions and hawksbeard – both are safe and eaten the same way.
MONTH SPAN:	Flowers June - September, hz 5, seeds ripen July - September

FOOD IDEAS:	Use like you would dandelions but the good thing is the leaves are not as bitter. Use in winter salads, blanch them, put them in pies or use the edible flowers for decoration.

Do you remember crystallized angelica from when your gran used to bake cakes? Such a pity it seems to have died out – let's give it a come back! So easy to do, cut the big fat stems of angelica, peel the outer skin off and discard. Cut the stems in to skinny matchstick sized pieces. Pop them in a saucepan and cover with equal amounts of water and sugar and simmer gently. Keep an eye on it so the sugar doesn't catch. As it gets thick and gloopy, tip it out onto greaseproof paper. If it hardens, leave it and tease the pieces apart when dry but still pliable. If still wet, sprinkle liberally with caster sugar to dry it out. Use to nibble on (it is meant to stop you craving alcohol) or use as cake decorations.

ANGELICA

Angelica archangelica

SYNONYM:	*Angelica officinalis*
NAME ORIGIN:	Literally means heavenly! Angelica helps with extreme labour, relieves cravings for alcohol and the qualities of the plant were said to be revealed by an angel. This angel also said it could cure the plague! Usually in seed on the feast day of St Michael - 29th September.
FAMILY:	**Apiaceae**
EDIBLE PART:	Stems, young leaves, seeds, roots
EDIBILITY RATING:	4
WHERE IT'S FOUND:	Shady moist ground, in gardens
LOOKALIKES:	Beware of lookalikes as it is in the Apiaceae family which contains many similar looking plants.
CAUTIONS:	Not recommended for pregnant women, contains furocoumarins which can cause photosensitivity to sunlight.
MONTH SPAN:	Flowers July - August, seeds ripen August - September. Biennial plant (Hz 4)
FOOD IDEAS:	Angelica seeds are used as a flavouring in liqueurs such as Chartreuse, a tea can be made from the leaves, the leaves can be added to dishes such as rhubarb, to give a sweet aniseed flavour, the peeled stems can be eaten raw or cooked, the root can be cooked and eaten.

BRACKEN
Pteridium aquilinum

SYNONYM:	*Pteris aquilina*
NAME ORIGIN:	*Pteris* is the Greek for wing as the branching fronds resemble wings and *aquilinum/aquilina* means eagle. Bracken comes from the Anglo-Saxon word *brake* meaning uncultivated land.
FAMILY:	Polypodiaceae

EDIBLE PART:	Young croziers
EDIBILITY RATING:	2
WHERE IT'S FOUND:	Heathland, moorland and acid woodland
CAUTIONS:	Beware of chemical spraying as it is very invasive and is sprayed to control it, plus the leaves are said to be carcinogenic and the leaves and roots contain thiaminase which if not cooked and properly prepared can deplete the body of Vitamin B1.
MONTH SPAN:	(Hz 4) Fronds emerge in May, spores ripen July - August

FOOD IDEAS:	Boil for about 10 minutes, discard the water and repeat - this leaches out the toxins making it safe to eat (see cautions). Use it as a vegetable or fry it up as a snack or side vegetable
OTHER INFO:	Bracken can be quite harmful to grazing animals. It is highly carcinogenic in its natural state causing bladder and intestinal tumours in them. Dad told me Great Granny Ball used to cook fiddleheads so on a memorable walk along the coastal path from Lelant to St Ives (age 11) I picked some fiddleheads and took them back to our house 'Driftwood' and cooked them. They were surprisingly delicious and very much like mushrooms.

PEA, FETA AND MINT CROQUETTES

(serves 2 as a starter.)

2 cups frozen peas
1 good handful mint leaves
2 tbsp diced feta
1 medium potato peeled, boiled and mashed
flour to combine and dust
crème fraiche
seasoning
olive oil to shallow fry

In a saucepan, get some water boiling and cook the peas until just cooked, roughly 5 minutes. In a bowl, mix together the feta, mashed potato and seasoning. Finely chop the mint and fold in carefully along with the peas until combined - try not to mash the peas. Using 2 dessert spoons, make quenelle shapes which is done by passing the mixture from one spoon to the other so it has three sides. Dust in flour and shallow fry on all three sides until golden. Serve with a little creme fraiche.

MINT
Mentha sp.

CORN MINT
Mentha arvensis

NAME ORIGIN:	*Menthe* is a Greek nymph, *arvensis* means field.
FAMILY:	Lamiaceae
EDIBLE PART:	Leaves and stems
EDIBILITY RATING:	5
WHERE IT'S FOUND:	Mints are garden plants or garden escapees, corn mint likes damp ground, arable land
LOOKALIKES:	Other plants in the Lamiaceae family so tear a leaf and smell to see if it's minty.
CAUTIONS:	A strong abortifacient and emmenagogue so avoid during pregnancy.
MONTH SPAN:	Corn mint flowers from May - October (Hz 4). Mint is usually in leaf from April onwards

FOOD IDEAS:	Use leaves raw in salads, to make sauces, jelly, or cooked in meals with meat, fish, vegetarian, rice, etc. tea from dried leaves. Works well as savoury or sweet dishes (Corn mint has a slight bitterness).
OTHER INFO:	Mint is very invasive, grow it in a pot if you want to grow it in your garden, and sink the pot into the ground (this acts as a root barrier).

PLAICE
Pleuronectes platessa

NAME ORIGIN:	The word *platessa* possibly comes from the word for plate, referring to the flat plate-like shape of the fish.
FAMILY:	**Pleuronectidae**

EDIBLE PART:	Flesh
EDIBILITY RATING:	5
WHERE IT'S FOUND:	Sea, off sandy and shingle beaches (also over mussel beds)
CAUTIONS:	Avoid if you have seafood allergies.
LOOKALIKES:	There are other flat fish but you can recognise plaice with its orange spots on its brown top. Flounder are similar but are missing the bony bumps that are on the head of plaice.
MONTH SPAN:	Spring, summer, autumn. It is best from late spring - early summer

FOOD IDEAS:	Fry, grill, bake.
OTHER INFO:	To catch plaice from the shore, use a 4-6oz beachcaster with bottom ledgered bait as this is where they dwell. Bait – lugworm and squid.

beads   swivel

swivel

weight

hooks

beads as attractors

PLAICE WITH HERB CRUSTY TOPPING
(serves 4)

4 skinned and filleted plaice fillets
1 1/4 cup breadcrumbs
1/2 cup flat leaf parsley
2 cloves garlic
zest of 1 lemon
seasoning
olive oil
salad and new potatoes to serve

Very simply whizz up the breadcrumbs, parsley, garlic cloves, lemon zest and seasoning in a food processor. On a baking tray, drizzle olive oil on the base and rub it around before laying the plaice fillets on it. Top each fillet with the herb breadcrumb mix so completely covered, then drizzle olive oil on the breadcrumbs. Pop under the grill from cold and grill - keep checking until the top is a rich brown colour and lift a corner of a fillet to see that it is cooked. If the crumbs are becoming too brown, drape a piece of tinfoil over the fish. Serve with salad and new potatoes and either a mayonnaise or a light creamy sauce (optional).

ATLANTIC MACKEREL
Scomber scombrus

FAMILY:	**Scombridae**
EDIBLE PART:	Meat
EDIBILITY RATING:	5
WHERE IT'S FOUND	Off a boat, pier, off the rocks or off the beach
CAUTIONS:	Avoid if you have allergies to seafood.
MONTH SPAN:	All year round in South West, April - October rest of UK

FOOD IDEAS:	Gut and fillet the fish, then barbecue or pan fry. You can bake it but don't let it dry out so maybe do it en papillote. If barbecuing, use a sharp knife and make 3 or 4 cross cuts and rub thyme, garlic, olive oil and sea salt into the incisions. Serve with gooseberry sauce or knotweed sauce. Why not have a go at making a smoker, then you can smoke your own mackerel for making pâté! Try it raw, sushi style.
	Have a look at Japanese knotweed jam recipe (May 1st) - this goes perfectly with barbecued mackerel - very simple, very tasty!
OTHER INFO:	Mackerel move inshore and north in spring, south in winter. The coolest thing, they belong to the Scombrini Tribe!! Mackerel are pelagic (wandering) which means they will swim anywhere for a meal. Other fish tend to stick to one depth or area. When catching mackerel, they use their sight so anything shiny works; a sliver of mackerel or sand eel with their silvery skin works well as bait!
	To catch mackerel you can use feathers, floats and spinners.

CHARLOCK

Sinapis arvensis

SYNONYM:	*Brassica arvensis, Brassica kaber, Brassica sinapis, Brassica sinapistrum*
NAME ORIGIN:	*Sinapis* derives from the Greek work *sinapi* which means mustard and *arvensis* means of the fields.
FAMILY:	**Brassicaceae**

EDIBLE PART:	Flowers, leaves, seed (oil)
EDIBILITY RATING:	2
WHERE IT'S FOUND:	Cultivated ground, pest weed of spring crops
LOOKALIKES:	Other brassicas! White mustard (*Sinapis alba*) has lobed smaller leaves (both edible).
CAUTIONS:	One source suggests the plant becomes poisonous once the seed pods have formed, but I haven't found this in any other source of information.
MONTH SPAN:	Flowers May - July, seeds ripen May - August

FOOD IDEAS:	Leaves raw or cooked. Try the young leaves in salads, older ones cooked as a 'green', young seed pods pickled or eaten raw, flowers raw, young shoots (flowering shoots) cooked and eaten as a vegetable.

SCOTS PINE

Pinus sylvestris

SYNONYM:	*Pinus rubra*
NAME ORIGIN:	*Pinus* is the ancient name for pine and *sylvestris* means of the woods.
FAMILY:	Pinaceae
EDIBLE PART:	Pollen, inner bark
EDIBILITY RATING:	2
WHERE IT'S FOUND:	Woodland, especially in Scotland
MONTH SPAN:	Flowers May, evergreen
CAUTIONS:	The resin and wood have been known to cause dermatitis in people with sensitive skin.

FOOD IDEAS:	Inner bark can be dried and ground to a powder to make bread.
OTHER INFO:	Scots pine is grown commercially for timber and is an important tree in its ecosystem for lichen, mosses, insects, birds, animals, plants and fungi including chanterelles.

MAIDENHAIR FERN

Adiantum capillus-veneris

NAME ORIGIN:	In Greek *a* means no and *diantos* means moistened as the leaves remain dry even when water is on them. *Capillus veneris* means Venus' hair referring to the shape of the leaves - think about it!
FAMILY:	**Polypodiaceae**

EDIBLE PART:	Leaves
EDIBILITY RATING:	2
WHERE IT'S FOUND:	Damp areas, rocks, walls, crevices, can cope with coastal conditions
CAUTIONS:	Emmenagogue, said to be abortifacient so avoid during pregnancy. Many ferns contain thiaminase which can cause beri beri and deplete the body's vitamin B complex. It has not been reported with this fern but best to be careful, and as long as you have a healthy balanced diet, should be no problem.
MONTH SPAN:	(Hz 9) Frost tender, in leaf May

FOOD IDEAS:	Dried leaves to decorate food and make tea or syrup.
OTHER INFO:	This fern has been used to make a cough syrup and a tea for menstrual cramps.

GROUND ELDER

goutweed

Aegopodium podagraria

NAME ORIGIN:	The Greek word *aigos* means goat and *podos* or *pous* means foot. The Latin word *podagra* means gout, hence the name.
FAMILY:	**Apiaceae**

EDIBLE PART:	Leaves and stems
EDIBILITY RATING:	3
WHERE IT'S FOUND:	Dappled shade, hedgerow, grassy area (light shade)
LOOKALIKES:	Dog's mercury *Mercurialis perennis* which is toxic and grows in similar places to ground elder, but is hairy.
MONTH SPAN:	Flowers May - July (Hz 5)

FOOD IDEAS:	Wash, add 1 tbsp of water and 1 tbsp of butter to a saucepan and add the ground elder, cook for 5-10 mins, season and eat as a vegetable - delicious. Nick likes the leaves but finds the stems are too much like Alexanders for him (I like them!). Not good in quiche by themselves. Try in soup with other spring greens, or in omelette.
OTHER INFO:	I'm so easily excited, aren't I? Oh well! Spotted this growing for the first time when Gill, Tiana and I went to Kent to Sissinghurst and Perch Hill for Sarah Raven's cut flower course. Little did I realise, I'd been sitting on it year after year a little closer to home!!! For years we would do a show garden at Boconnoc Spring Show and every time, we would spend our lunch sitting on a stone wall, gazing wistfully at the stunning countryside (we'd pretend we owned all that we surveyed). If I'd gazed wistfully towards my feet I would have noticed ground elder had been growing there all along! Introduced by the Romans along with Alexanders, it's a pretty invasive plant but one of the more delicious ones that once you've tasted, you'll be happy for it to take over your garden! I would! I'm stuck with bindweed and boring *Equisetum scorpioides* which is not edible! Monks used to grow the plant in monasteries to cure gout.

COLUMBINE
Aquilegia vulgaris

NAME ORIGIN:	*Aquila* means eagle as the flower looks like an eagle claw and *columba* from the Latin for dove.
FAMILY:	Ranunculaceae

EDIBLE PART:	Flowers, leaves
EDIBILITY RATING:	2
WHERE IT'S FOUND:	Shade, moist ground
CAUTIONS:	The roots are toxic but cooking or drying them destroys the toxin.
MONTH SPAN:	Flowers April - July, seeds ripen July - August hz 4

FOOD IDEAS:	Eat the sweet flowers raw or make a tea from them. Eat the young fresh leaves in salads.

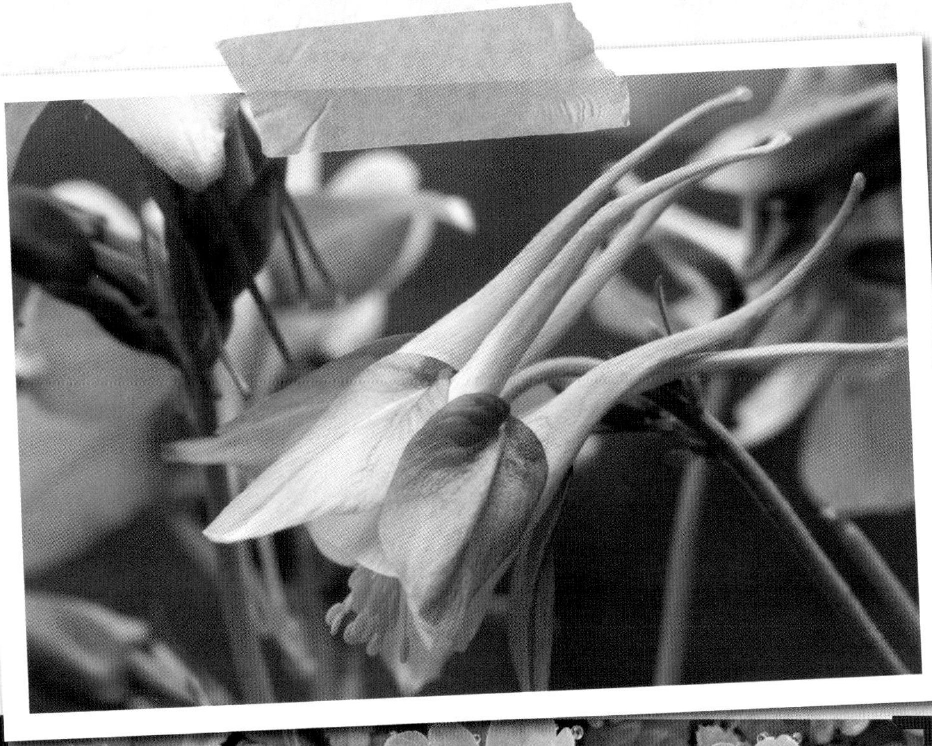

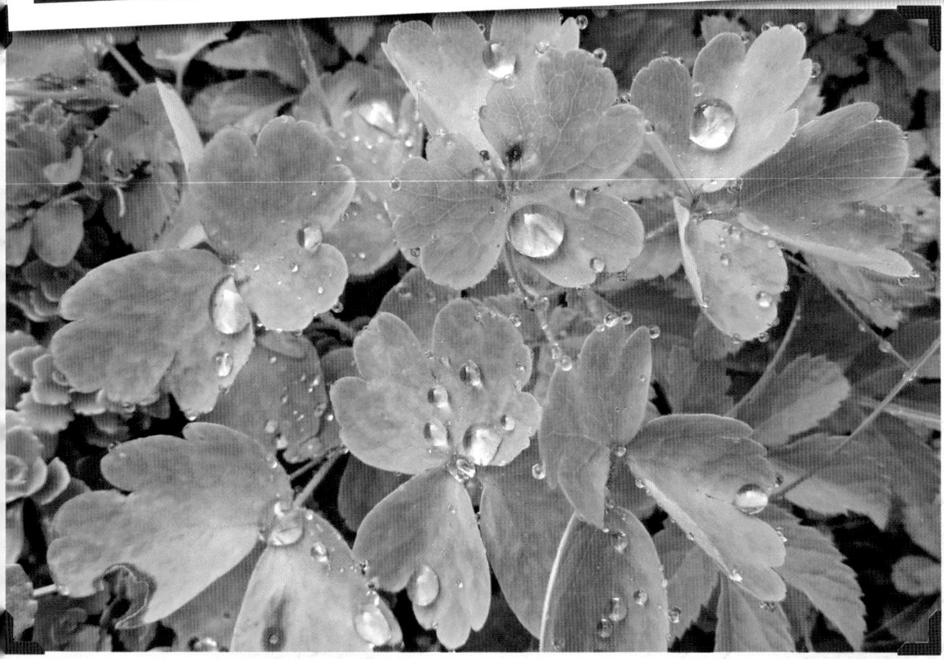

BABINGTON'S LEEK

Allium ampeloprasum **var.** *babingtonii*

SYNONYM:	*Allium babingtonii*
NAME ORIGIN:	*All* is Celtic for burning and pungent and *prasum* is old Greek for leek.
FAMILY:	Amaryllidaceae
EDIBLE PART:	Bulb, bulbils, leaves
EDIBILITY RATING:	4
WHERE IT'S FOUND:	Coastal areas, sandy soil
CAUTIONS:	All Alliums are toxic to dogs.
LOOKALIKES:	Daffodils *Narcissus* sp. look similar before they flower but a torn daffodil leaf has no onion/garlic smell whereas alliums do.
MONTH SPAN:	In leaf from January

FOOD IDEAS:	Eat the bulb, bulbils and leaves raw or cooked, use it like a leek. You can pickle the bulbils. Use it in soups, stews, pasta dishes, salads, any savoury dish you normally use onions or leeks.
OTHER INFO:	It is one of our native alliums that likes to grow near the coast. The leaves can be eaten from January. It is useful as a companion plant by making the other plant more resilient against pests and diseases, except for brassicas.

Why not try homemade pizza topped with Babington's leeks and something like prosciutto and rosemary?

BLACK LOCUST

Robinia pseudoacacia

NAME ORIGIN:	Named after Jean Robin, a French botanist and herbalist to Henry IV of France. The species means false acacia because it looks similar to acacia (same family).
FAMILY:	Fabaceae

EDIBLE PART:	Flowers and cooked seeds
EDIBILITY RATING:	2
WHERE IT'S FOUND:	Woodland, thicket
CAUTIONS:	All but the flowers are toxic, but the toxin is destroyed by heat making the seeds edible.
LOOKALIKES:	Not to be confused with honey locust (*Gleditsia* sp.).
MONTH SPAN:	Flowers late May, seeds ripen November - March

FOOD IDEAS:	Boil the seeds and eat them like peas.

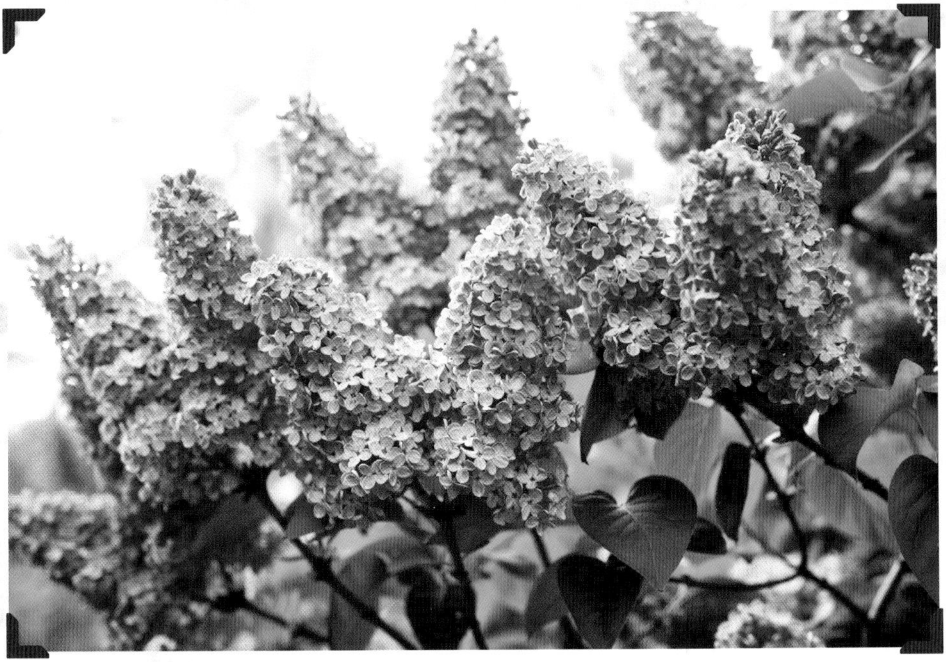

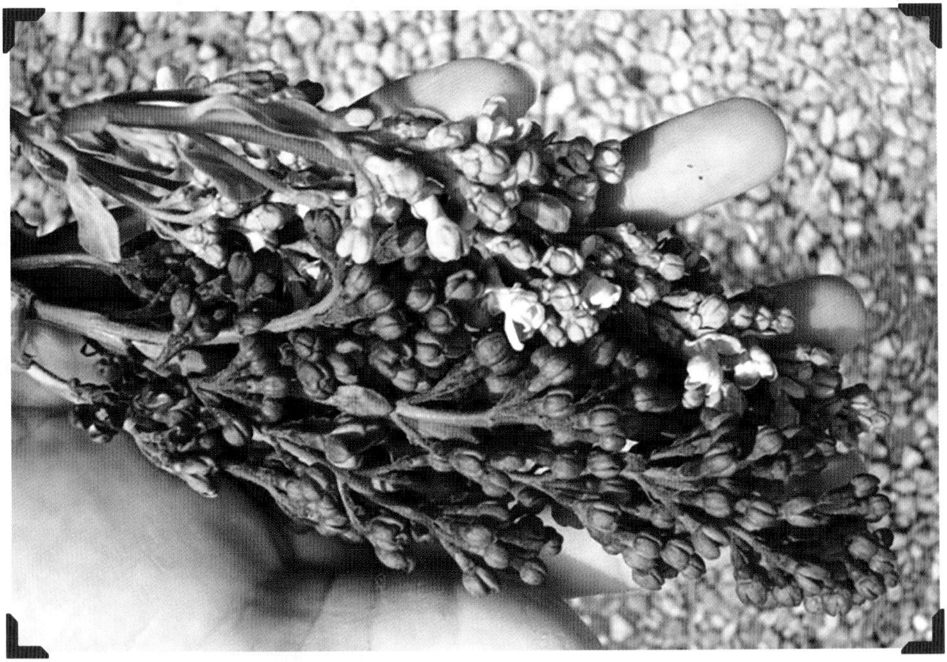

LILAC

Syringa vulgaris

NAME ORIGIN:	The Greek word *syrinx* means tubes as the stems are hollow and sometimes used as pipe stems. *Vulgaris* means common.
FAMILY:	Oleaceae

EDIBLE PART:	Flowers
EDIBILITY RATING:	2
WHERE IT'S FOUND:	Gardens, hedgerows
MONTH SPAN:	(Hz 5) flowers May

FOOD IDEAS:	Flowers raw or dipped in a tempura batter and deep fried, dusted with icing sugar. Slight bitterness probably from the stalk, so another way is to strip the flowers off with a fork and mix it into the batter and fry. Make a simple tempura batter with a light lager or with cider.
OTHER INFO:	The flower fritters taste very much like parma violets and wine and conjure up images of English meadows, head high ox-eye daisies, petticoats and a glass of something ice cold under the shade of an oak tree!

"LILAC WINE, I FEEL UNSTEADY, WHERE'S MY LOVE LISTEN TO ME, WHY IS EVERYTHING SO HAZY ISN'T THAT SHE, OR AM I JUST GOING CRAZY, DEAR LILAC WINE, I FEEL UNREADY FOR MY LOVE, "

Jeff Buckley, Lilac Wine

DRYAD'S SADDLE

Polyporus squamosus

NAME ORIGIN:	*Polyporus* means many holes relating to the pores on the underside of this bracket fungus.
	The name dryad's saddle comes from the Greek mythological nymphs called dryads who could feasibly sit on and ride this fungus as they get to a substantial size. *Squamosus* comes from the word squamules meaning scales.
FAMILY:	Polyporaceae
EDIBLE PART:	Mushroom
EDIBILITY RATING:	3
WHERE IT'S FOUND:	Deciduous trees, especially beech, elm and sycamore.
CAUTIONS:	Unknown
MONTH SPAN:	Spring - summer

FOOD IDEAS:	Dried and powdered, then used in soups, pasta and casseroles to flavour. Finely slice and fry but check for maggots and choose young specimens. They smell like lemony squash balls!
OTHER INFO:	This is the only bracket fungus with pores, white flesh and dark brown scales. Paper can be made from this genus of fungus.

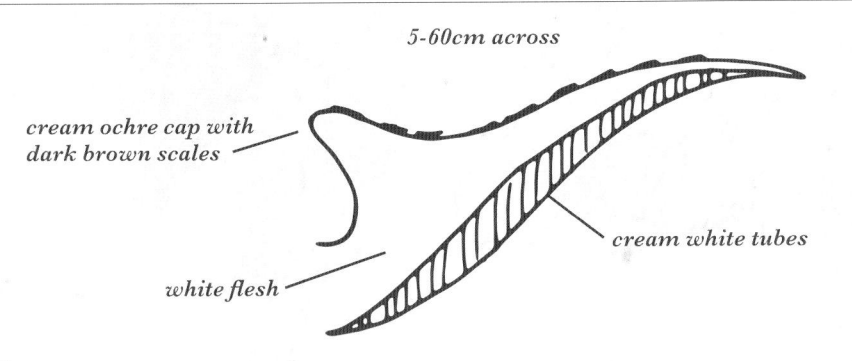

5-60cm across

cream ochre cap with dark brown scales

cream white tubes

white flesh

GYPSYWORT

Lycopus europaeus

SYNONYM:	*Lycopus alboroseus, Lycopus albus, Lycopus aquaticus, Lycopus decrescens*
NAME ORIGIN:	*Lycos* means wolf and *europaeus* means from Europe. Gypsywort is so-named as gypsies would dye their skin and clothes with it.
FAMILY:	**Lamiaceae**
EDIBLE PART:	Root
EDIBILITY RATING:	I
WHERE IT'S FOUND:	Damp meadows, by streams, ditches, fens
LOOKALIKES:	It looks similar to mint as it has square stems and opposite leaves, but without the mint smell.
CAUTIONS:	Avoid if pregnant, or have hypothyroidism as it is known to cause enlargement of the thyroid gland.
MONTH SPAN:	(Hz 5) flowers June - September, seeds August - October

FOOD IDEAS:	Eat the root raw or cooked.
OTHER INFO:	First saw this on 'The Meadows' across the river from the city of Chester, where I attended secondary school. In my later teens, it was the place to go and party, but at all ages I'd walk around the meadows which nestle in the curve of the river Dee and take photos, go sledging in winter, play frisbee on my birthday, lose the frisbee the first time we used it by flinging it into someone's garden...AND occasionally finding a new plant such as gypsywort.

MUSK MALLOW
Malva moschata

NAME ORIGIN:	*Malakos* is Greek for soft and soothing and *moschata* means musk.
FAMILY:	Malvaceae

EDIBLE PART:	Leaf (flower)
EDIBILITY RATING:	3
WHERE IT'S FOUND:	Meadows, grassland, banks
LOOKALIKES:	Other mallows look similar but the leaf shape is a good indicator.
CAUTIONS:	Only if the plant is growing in nitrogen rich soil does it obtain high concentrations of nitrates in the leaves.
MONTH SPAN:	Flowers July - August, seeds ripen August - September (Hz 3) Leaves available from spring (April)

FOOD IDEAS:	Flowers raw, leaves raw or cooked - good salad substitute or add to soups or stews to thicken sauce, raw immature seeds as a snack.
OTHER INFO:	All mallows are mucilaginous and are therefore soothing to a sore throat.

TOASTED PIGNUT AND PIGNUT SALAD

No real recipe here but either scrape clean and wash the pignuts, then slice. Mix in a bowl with seasonal salad leaves and flowers and dress with a light lemony dressing. If you toast the pignuts under the grill until they start to show colour, to me they taste like sweet chestnuts, so eat them as a snack or coat them in maple syrup and roast a little more with a small pinch of sea salt to bring out the flavour.

PIGNUT

Conopodium majus

SYNONYM:	*Bunium flexuosum, Conopodium denudatum*
NAME ORIGIN:	*Konos* is Greek for cone and pod means foot. It is called pignut because of its edible tubers that grow underground.
FAMILY:	Apiaceae

EDIBLE PART:	Tuber
EDIBILITY RATING:	4
WHERE IT'S FOUND:	Fields, banks, hedgerows, semi-shade
LOOKALIKES:	Other plants in Apiaceae family, so careful identification is a must.
MONTH SPAN:	Flowers May-June (seeds ripen July - August)

FOOD IDEAS:	Dig up with your nails, scrape off and eat as it is! Otherwise, cook and it tastes like a chestnut. I love these as a snack.
OTHER INFO:	Pignut is fantastic! My mate Fi would always tell me about country walks and digging up pignut, and until 10 years ago, I'd been completely oblivious to this plant. I'd seen it in books but never seen it for real so was unsure of the scale and most Apiaceae family are difficult to identify. A few years ago, Cath and I dug up our first pignut tuber and WOW what a corker!! It was massive, I later found out, compared to the norm!

EYEBRIGHT
Euphrasia officinalis

SYNONYM:	*Bartsia imbricata*
NAME ORIGIN:	*Eu* is Greek for good or well and *officinalis* means of the shop (medicinal).
FAMILY:	Scrophulariaceae

EDIBLE PART:	Leaves
EDIBILITY RATING:	I
WHERE IT'S FOUND:	Grassland, pastures (chalk soil) semi-parasitic plant
CAUTIONS:	The only caution is in eye use as it possibly causes headaches, sensitivity to light and swelling.
MONTH SPAN:	(Hz 6) flowers July - September

FOOD IDEAS:	Eat the leaves raw in salads although they are quite bitter.
OTHER INFO:	Eyebright was used as an eye wash by monks who would get sore eyes as their only light was candle light, which would cause eye strain (not recommended now due to side effects). All Euphrasias are classed as an endangered species and are protected, so must never be uprooted.

RAPE

Brassica napus (napus)

NAME ORIGIN:	*Rapa* is the name for turnip and *bresic* is Celtic meaning cabbage.
FAMILY:	**Brassicaceae**

EDIBLE PART:	Seed, sprouted seed, leaves, young flowering stems
EDIBILITY RATING:	2
WHERE IT'S FOUND:	Fields, ditches, damp areas
LOOKALIKES:	Other brassicas look very similar including charlock *Sinapis arvensis* but both can be eaten.
MONTH SPAN:	(Hz 7) flowers May - August
CAUTIONS:	Modern cultivars have mostly bred out the toxic erucic acid from the seed oil. If concerned avoid eating the seeds.

FOOD IDEAS:	Eat the leaves raw or cooked, cooked flowering stems, seeds.
OTHER INFO:	Rapeseed oil is being used more and more in cooking as it has a very mild flavour which doesn't detract from the flavours of the dish. Unfortunately people can have an allergic reaction to this, sometimes similar to hay fever. Canola oil and what is classed as 'vegetable oil' is mostly rapeseed oil, because it is inexpensive to produce.

HEUCHERA alum root
Heuchera sp.

NAME ORIGIN:	The genus is named after the German botanist Johann Heinreich Von Heucher. The family name comes from the words Saxon meaning rock and *frango* meaning I break as this family tends to grow well on rocks or in rocky fissures with deep penetrating roots.
FAMILY:	Saxifragaceae

EDIBLE PART:	Leaves
EDIBILITY RATING:	3
LOOKALIKES:	*Tiarella* sp. looks similar – this is a rockery plant with unknown edibility. Heuchera leaves are broader and tiarella leaves are more palmate with delicate little white flowers on a stalk.
WHERE IT'S FOUND:	Gardens, woodland, dappled shade
MONTH SPAN:	Perennial in leaf from about March

FOOD IDEAS:	Raw or cooked leaves
	Some heuchera species/cultivars taste like cucumbers and make a great addition to salads and they look great too!
OTHER INFO:	Bramble my puppy taught me you can eat heuchera leaves! He is a natural born forager and when he started munching on them in my garden, I wondered if they were safe for human consumption. Bramble knows his stuff, he likes to eat figs, courgette leaves, wild strawberries and vine leaves from the garden! A few years ago, I won gold and best in show for 'the living room' where everything was made out of plants including the armchairs that were planted up with thousands of heuchera plug plants... never again! They did look fab though! One of its common names is alum root as the roots can be used as an alum substitute and work as a mordant for fixing dyes.

COW PARSLEY

wild chervil

Anthriscus sylvestris

NAME ORIGIN:	*Anthriscus* is the Greek name of this genus named by Pliny and *sylvestris* means of the woods.
FAMILY:	**Apiaceae**
EDIBLE PART:	Leaves
EDIBILITY RATING:	2
WHERE IT'S FOUND:	Hedgerows, woodland edge
LOOKALIKES:	Hemlock *Conium maculatum*! Very poisonous! Hemlock flowers from June - July and has purple blotches on the stems where cow parsley can have purple tinged stems but never blotchy.
CAUTIONS:	It contains toxic phenolic compounds which are extremely violent abortives and it has a drastic effect on the uterus
MONTH SPAN:	Flowers April - June

FOOD IDEAS:	I think this is over-rated but it can be used as a garnish, or for a sauce or dressing, instead of parsley, but it lacks the flavour. Goes quite well with beetroot due to its earthiness. Don't bother cooking it as it loses its flavour.
OTHER INFO:	Chervil is *Anthriscus cerefolium*, so closely related, hence the name wild chervil.

SEA MILKWEED
black saltwort, sea milkwort

Glaux maritima

NAME ORIGIN:	*Maritima* **means maritime or of the sea and** *Glaux* **is the Greek for owl.**
FAMILY:	**Primulaceae (Myrsinaceae)**

EDIBLE PART:	Shoots, roots
EDIBILITY RATING:	2
WHERE IT'S FOUND:	Estuaries, salt marshes, full sun
LOOKALIKES:	Looks like a mound of thyme but with no smell.
MONTH SPAN:	Flowers June - August

FOOD IDEAS:	Eat the young shoots raw or cooked, boiled or roasted. The roots can possibly make you sleepy. Under milkweed rather than milkwood!
OTHER INFO:	I first saw this growing along the Gannel river at Newquay and thought it was thyme, but because it had no smell, I wasn't sure what it was… later finding it to be Glaux maritima. A new discovery! Very late to emerge and has little pink flowers.

THAI RELISH

1 tbsp water
4 tbsp rice wine vinegar
4 tsp caster sugar
a pinch of salt
4 cups of ice plant leaves,
finely sliced
2 shallots, peeled and sliced
1 medium chilli, finely sliced
2 tbsp fresh coriander, sliced

Simmer the vinegar, water, sugar and salt together in a saucepan until the sugar has dissolved. Leave to cool. When cool, add the remaining ingredients, cover with cling film and pop in the fridge to marinade. Serve with chicken skewers or thai fish cakes.

ICE PLANT
Sedum spectabile

SYNONYM:	*Hylotelephium spectabile*
NAME ORIGIN:	The genus *Sedum* comes from the Latin word *sedar* meaning to calm (think sedate) from the healing properties of certain Sedums and *spectabile* means showy or striking referring to the colourful flowers.
FAMILY:	Crassulaceae

EDIBLE PART:	Leaves
EDIBILITY RATING:	2
WHERE IT'S FOUND:	Gardens, damp woodland edges, garden escapee
CAUTIONS:	None known
LOOKALIKES:	Other sedums look similar but all have edible leaves, although eat those with yellow flowers in moderation.
MONTH SPAN:	Young shoots appear from January/February, flowers in September (Hz 6)

FOOD IDEAS:	Eat the leaves raw or cooked. They have a mild slightly peppery flavour and if eaten raw they can be sliced up or eaten whole, in dips or as an addition to salads.
OTHER INFO:	The ice plant produces beautiful solid flower clusters in dusky hot pinks which make an excellent addition to an autumn flower arrangement because of their late flowering but they also hold their colour and dry quite well too. A great plant for bees.

BEETROOT AND PINK PURSLANE SALAD WITH SMOKED MACKEREL
(serves 4)

3 smoked mackerel fillets,
skinned and de-boned
4 cooked beetroot, chopped
or sliced
150g pink purslane leaves plus
flowers to garnish

Dressing
6 tbsp olive oil
2 tbsp white wine vinegar
juice and zest of half a lemon
1 garlic clove, peeled and finely
chopped
2 tsp horseradish cream
sea salt and black pepper

Make the dressing by combining the dressing ingredients. On 4 plates, equally serve out the beetroot and pink purslane leaves. Flake the mackerel into bite-sized chunks and add them to the plates. Drizzle the dressing over the salad and decorate with the pink purslane flowers.

" IN WILD WATER YOU ARE ON EQUAL TERMS WITH THE ANIMAL WORLD AROUND YOU: IN EVERY SENSE, ON THE SAME LEVEL."
Waterlog by Roger Deakin

PINK PURSLANE
Siberian purslane

Claytonia sibirica

SYNONYM:	*Claytonia alsinoides*
NAME ORIGIN:	*Claytonia* was named after John Clayton, an American plant collector. *Sibirica* means it originates from Siberia.
FAMILY:	**Portulacaceae**

EDIBLE PART:	Flowers and leaves
EDIBILITY RATING:	3
WHERE IT'S FOUND:	Riversides and stream edges
MONTH SPAN:	Evergreen (flowers April - July)
LOOKALIKES:	Other species of the edible Claytonia genus.
CAUTIONS:	Only caution is the water quality that it is growing by.

FOOD IDEAS:	Eat as a salad leaf or use the older leaves cooked as a vegetable. As a salad, the leaves are best mixed with other salad leaves and with a dressing. It goes well with the earthiness of beetroot. They are a good source of vitamin C.
OTHER INFO:	I found this for the first time at Respryn near Bodmin when walking with Gill, who was eyeing up the river for the best places for a spot of wild swimming.

TREAT WITH CAUTION

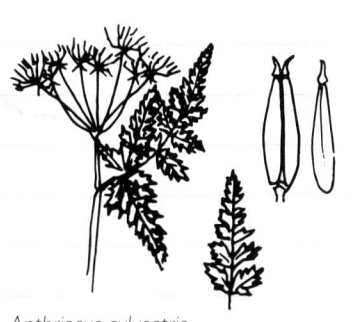

Anthriscus sylvestris
cow parsley
*can cause allergic reactions in some people

Pastinaca sativa
wild parsnip
*sap can cause photosensitivity/dermatitis

Apium nodiflorum
fool's watercress
*not poisonous, supposedly edible but not very pleasant

Heracleum sphondylium
hogweed
*sap can cause photosensitivity

Berula erecta
lesser water parsnip
*easily mistaken with water hemlock *Cicuta virosa*
(also known as cowbane)

Sium latifolium
greater water parsnip
*unpleasant

NON EDIBLES

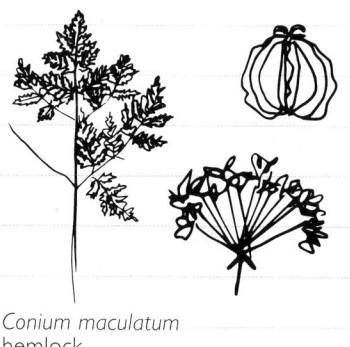

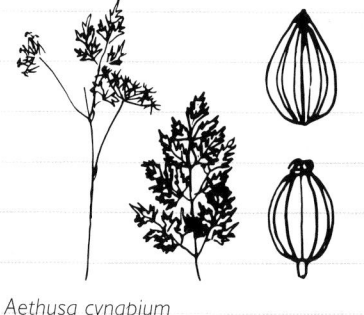

Conium maculatum
hemlock

Aethusa cynapium
fool's parsley

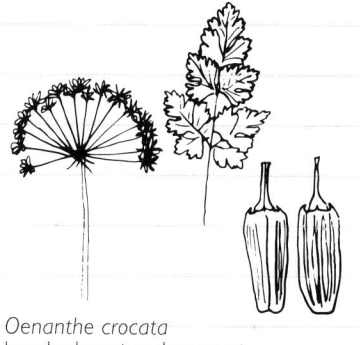

Oenanthe crocata
hemlock water dropwort

Oenanthe aquatica
water dropwort

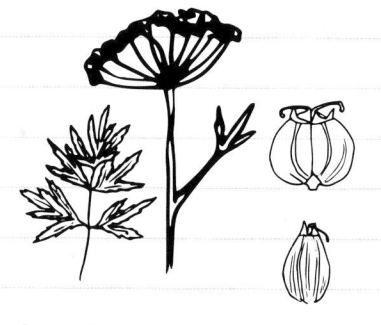

Cicuta virosa
cowbane

EDIBLES

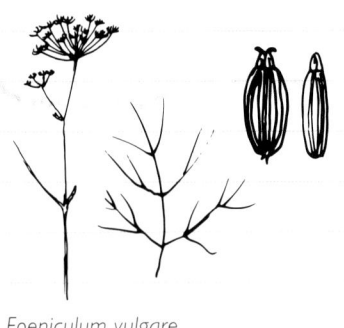

Foeniculum vulgare
fennel

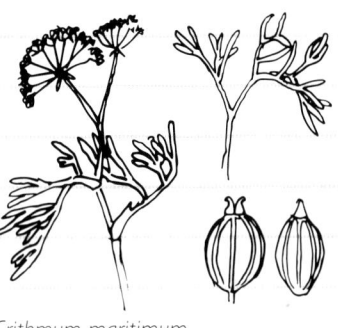

Crithmum maritimum
rock samphire

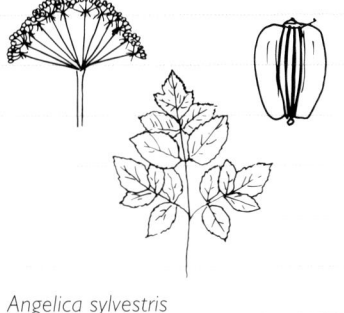

Angelica sylvestris
wild angelica

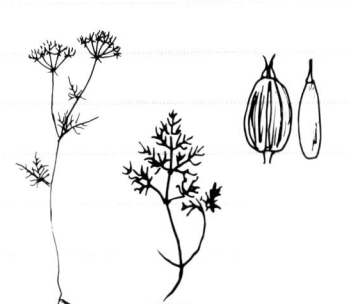

Conopodium majus
pignut

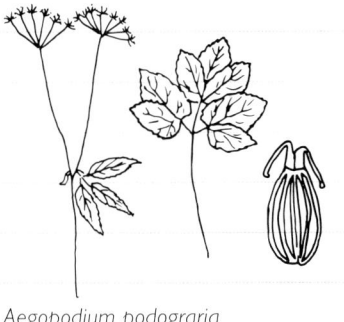

Aegopodium podograria
ground elder

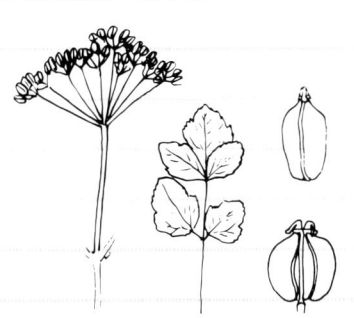

Smyrnium olusatrum
alexanders

Levisticum officinale
lovage

Eryngium maritimum
sea holly

Myrrhis odorata
sweet cicely

Angelica archangelica
angelica

Ligusticum scoticum
scots lovage

Daucus carota
wild carrot

MEDICAL TERMINOLOGY

abortifacient
(Chiefly of a drug) causing abortion.

acetic acid
The acid that gives vinegar its characteristic taste. The pure acid is a colourless viscous liquid or glassy solid. Alternative name: ethanoic acid; chemical formula: CH_3COOH

alkaloids
Any of a class of nitrogenous organic compounds of plant origin which have pronounced physiological actions on humans. They include many drugs (morphine, quinine) and poisons (atropine, strychnine).

anthocyanin
A blue, violet, or red flavonoid pigment found in plants.

anticoagulant
Having the effect of retarding or inhibiting the coagulation of the blood.

arthritis
A serious condition in which a person's joints become painful, swollen and stiff.

bio-mimicry
The design and production of materials, structures, and systems that are modelled on biological entities and processes.

carcinogens
A substance capable of causing cancer in living tissue.

coumarins
A vanilla-scented compound found in many plants, formerly used for flavouring food. A bicyclic lactone; chemical formula: $C_9H_6O_2$

dermatitis
A medical condition in which the skin becomes red, swollen, and sore, sometimes with small blisters, resulting from direct irritation of the skin by an external agent or an allergic reaction to it.

di-coumarins (dicoumarins)
Dicoumarin is a crystalline compound that is naturally formed from damp spoiled plants in the pea family (Fabaceae) which smelled sweet due to containing coumarins. Dicoumarin is a potent anticoagulant which if eaten causes spontaneous haemorrhaging.

emmenagogue
A substance that stimulates or increases menstrual flow.

erucic acid (Brassicaceae)
A solid compound present in mustard and rape seeds. An unsaturated fatty acid: chemical formula: $C_{21}H_{41}COOH$

farnesol
A natural compound present in many essential oils such as rose, citronella and tuberose which when isolated is used in the perfume industry to enhance sweet floral fragrances.

furocoumarins
Chemical substances that cause skin sensitivity to sunlight, which leave irregular pigmentation and skin prone to sunburn.

galactose
A sugar of the hexose class which is a constituent of lactose and many polysaccharides.

gamma-linolenic acid (GLA)
A polyunsaturated fatty acid (with one more double bond than linoleic acid) present as a glyceride in linseed and other oils and essential in the human diet.

gout
A build up of uric acid.

hydrogen cyanide
A highly poisonous gas or volatile liquid

with an odour of bitter almonds, made
by the action of acids on cyanides.
Chemical formula: HCN

hypothyroidism
Abnormally low activity of the thyroid gland,
resulting in retardation of growth
and mental development in children and
adults.

oxalic acid
A poisonous crystalline acid with a sour
taste, present in rhubarb leaves, wood
sorrel, and other plants. Alternative
name: **ethanedioic acid**; chemical
formula: $(COOH)_2$

phenothiazines
A synthetic compound which is used in
veterinary medicine to treat parasitic
infestations of animals. A heterocyclic
compound; chemical formula: $C_{12}H_9NS$

photosensitivity
To have a chemical, electrical or other
response to light.

pyrrolizidine alkaloids
A group of alkaloids produced by certain
plant families to protect the plant from
insect herbivore damage. Over consuming
can cause liver damage and damage to
other organs. It can also be a potential
cause of cancer.

rheumatism
A medical condition that causes stiffness and
pain in the joints or muscles of the body.

saponins
A toxic compound which is present in
certain plants such as soapwort and
makes foam when shaken with water.

sedative
A drug used to calm a person or animal or
to make them sleep.

thiaminase
An enzyme that destroys thiamine which
is vitamin B1. Deficiency can result in
beriberi - a disease that affects systems
of the body such as the nervous system
and digestive system.

thujone
A chemical with a menthol odour found
in certain conifers and plants such as tansy,
artemisia and sage. Thujone is a stimulant
and convulsant in large quantities.

trimethylamine
An organic compound produced by the
decomposition of plants and animals -
the smell of death.

trypsin inhibitors
An inhibitor of trypsin - a digestive
enzyme which breaks down proteins
in the small intestine, secreted by the
pancreas as trypsinogen.

FOOD TERMINOLOGY

bain marie
A pan of hot water in which a cooking
container is placed for slow cooking.

crudités
Small pieces of uncooked vegetables,
often served with a dip before a meal.

en papillote
A food cooked and served in paper.

mirin
A rice wine used as a flavouring in Japanese
cookery.

wasabi
A Japanese plant with a thick green root
which tastes like strong horseradish and is
used in cookery, especially in powder or
paste form as an accompaniment to raw fish.

FISH AND SHELLFISH

carapace
The hard upper shell of a tortoise, crustacean, or arachnid.

pelagic
Fish that inhabit the many upper layers of the open sea. Mackerel are pelagic or wandering as they will go in search of food where most fish inhabit one layer and wait for food to come to them so as not to expend too much energy.

PLANT TERMINOLOGY

aerial parts
All parts of a plant growing above the ground.

annual
A plant that lives for a year or less, perpetuating itself by seed.

biennial
A plant that takes two years to grow from seed to fruition and die.

perennial
A plant that lives for several years.

bract
A modified leaf or scale, typically small, with a flower or flower cluster in its axil. Bracts are sometimes larger and more brightly coloured than the true flower, as in poinsettia.

calyx
The sepals of a flower, typically forming a whorl that encloses the petals and forms a protective layer around a flower in bud.

corymbs - like elderflower
A flower cluster whose lower stalks are proportionally longer so that the flowers form a flat or slightly convex head.

croziers
The curled top of a young fern, named after a hooked staff carried by a bishop.

fiddleheads
The young, curled, edible frond of certain ferns. Both fiddleheads and croziers refer to the same part.

cultivar
A plant variety that has been produced in cultivation by selective breeding. Cultivars are usually designated in the style *Taxus baccata* 'Variegata'.

variety
A taxonomic category that ranks below subspecies (where present) or species, its members differing from others of the same subspecies or species in minor but permanent or heritable characteristics. Varieties are more often recognized in botany, in which they are designated in the style *Apium graveolens* (var. **dulce**).

family
A principal taxonomic category that ranks above genus and below order, usually ending in *-idae* (in zoology) or *-aceae* (in botany).

genus
A principal taxonomic category that ranks above species and below family, and is denoted by a capitalized Latin name, e.g. *Helianthus*.

hz - hardiness zone
Hardiness of a plant depends on its ability to survive outside during winter.

sepals
Each of the parts of the calyx of a flower, enclosing the petals and typically green and leaf-like.

silicles
Disc-shaped seed pods of the Brassicaceae family.

species
A group of living organisms consisting of similar individuals capable of exchanging genes or interbreeding. The species is the principal natural taxonomic unit, ranking below a genus and denoted by a Latin binomial, e.g. *Helianthus annuus*.

stamen
The male fertilizing organ of a flower, typically consisting of a pollen-containing anther and a filament.

stigma
In a flower the part of a pistil that receives the pollen during pollination.

synonym
A taxonomic name which has the same application as another, especially one which has been superceded and is no longer valid.

whorl
A set of leaves, flowers, or branches springing from the stem at the same level and encircling it.

ROOTS

corm
A rounded underground storage organ present in plants such as croci, gladioli, and cyclamens, consisting of a swollen stem base covered with scale leaves.

rhizome
A continuously growing horizontal underground stem which puts out lateral shoots and adventitious roots at intervals.

bulb
A rounded underground storage organ present in some plants, notably those of the lily family, consisting of a short stem surrounded by fleshy scale leaves or leaf bases, lying dormant over winter.

FUNGI

adnate
Where the gills are attached to the stem.

decurrent
A fungus gill extending down the stem below the point of attachment.

free gills
Where the gills are not attached to the stem.

WINE MAKING

demi john
A bulbous narrow-necked bottle holding from 3 to 10 gallons of liquid.

fermenting
The chemical breakdown of a substance by bacteria, yeasts, or other microorganisms, typically involving effervescence and the giving off of heat. The fermentation process involved in the making of beers, wines, and spirits, in which sugars are converted to ethanol (ethyl alcohol). C_2H_5OH

racking
Siphoning alcohol away from the settled sediment to produce clear alcohol.

sediment
Matter that settles to the bottom of a liquid; dregs.

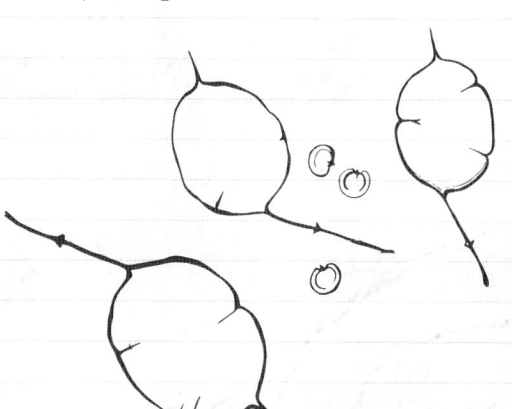

By scientific name A-Z

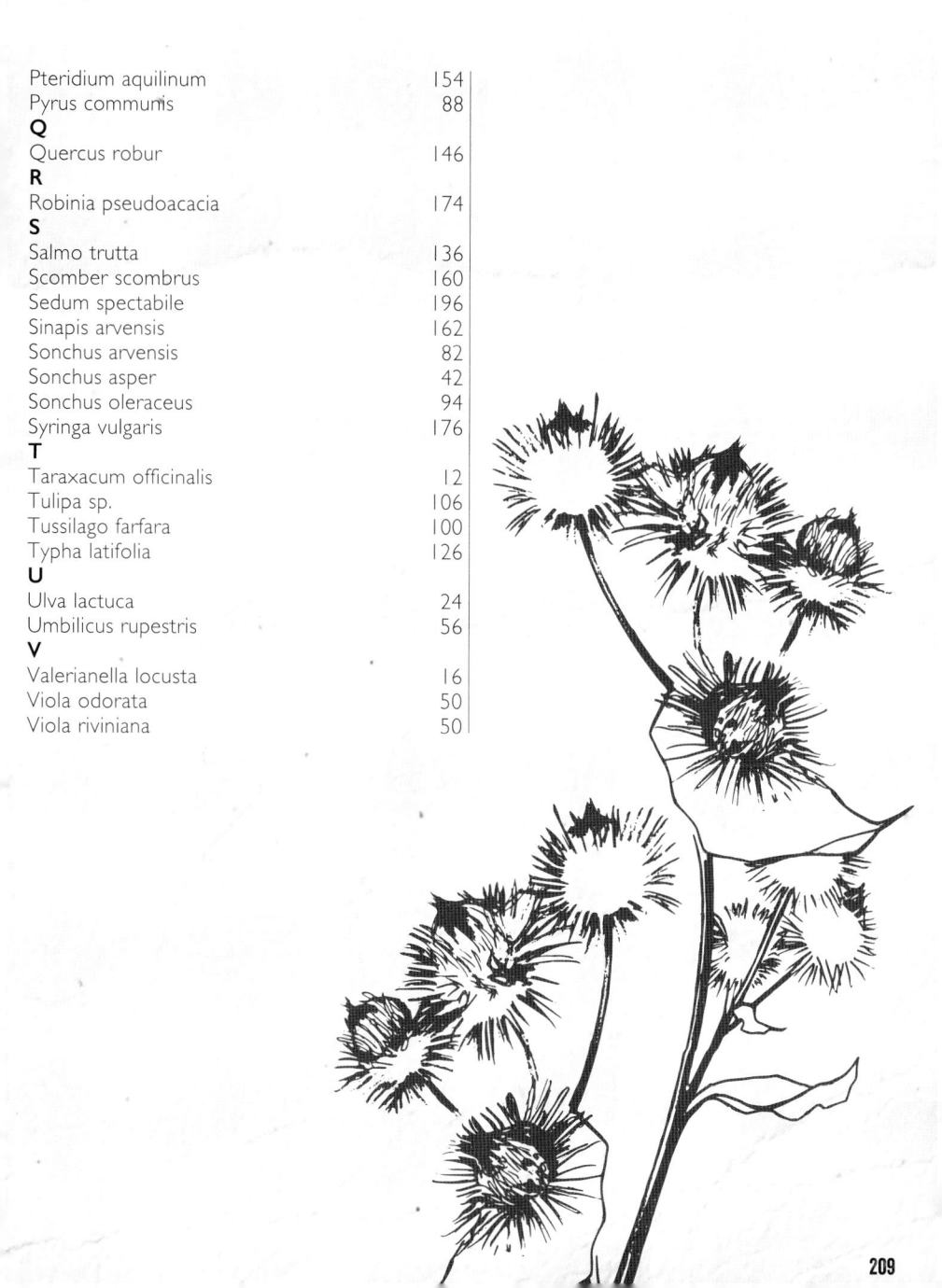

By common name A-Z

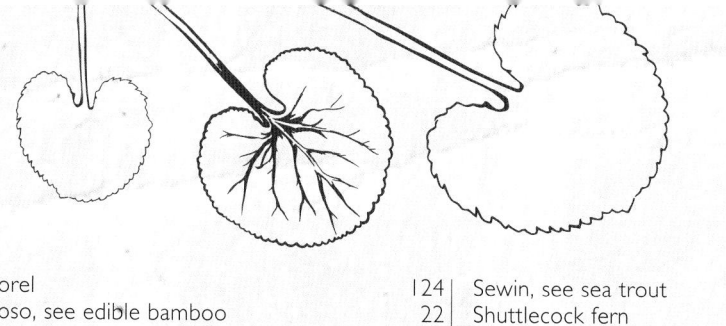

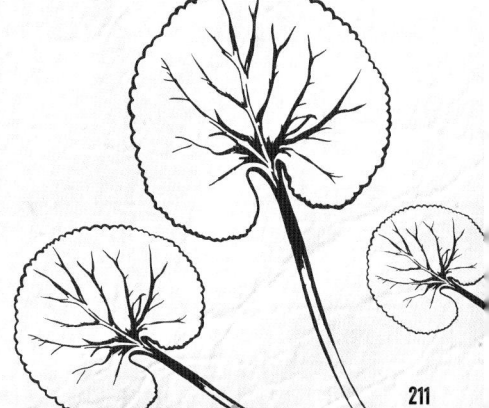

Acknowledgements

Graphic Design – Leap www.leap.uk.net
Illustration – Orlagh Murphy, Emma Gunn
Photographer – Emma Gunn
Proof-readers – Barbara Ball, Michael Ball, Emma Gunn
Fishing expert – Richard Buck www.fishandforage.co.uk

Picture credits

All photos are copyright of Emma Gunn, Shutterstock,
Jessy Edgar for Pteridium aquilinum, with the exception of
the following: Wikimedia - Mycelis muralis – Amadej Trnkoczy,
Montia fontana – abalg October 2008, Epilobium tetragonum
– Rasbak June 2005, Galium mollugo – H. Zell May 2009,
Coronopus didymus Rasbak July 2005, Coronopus squamatus
– Fornax January 2006, Ligusticum scoticum – Stemonitis August
2008, black squat lobster – Akuppa September 2007, Mentha
requienii – Michael XXLF July 2011.

Author Photograph: James Ram - chetwoderam.com - Chetwode
Ram - Commercial Photography | Still Life Photography

HOW TO DRESS A CRAB

No need to go in search of miniature clothing, you just need the following…
**a small hammer
a teaspoon
a metal skewer
chopping board
2 bowls
a sharp knife**

1. Put the crab upside down on the chopping board so its claws are facing up. Twist the claws and legs off and put to one side.

2. Put both your thumbs on the crab's tail and push the underside section up and off (this is the part which tells you whether it is male or female).

3. Remove the grey stomach sac (found behind the mouth) and dead man's fingers and discard.

4. Pick the meat out of the rest of the shell - put the brown meat in one bowl and the white meat in the other. Use the skewer to get all the meat out of every crevice.

5. Crack the claws and legs with the hammer and poke out the meat with the skewer and end of the teaspoon.

6. Use the hammer to crack off the underside shell of the main body so you are left with a neat rim. Rinse the shell and either put the brown meat in first then cover with the white meat, or put the white and brown meat side by side.

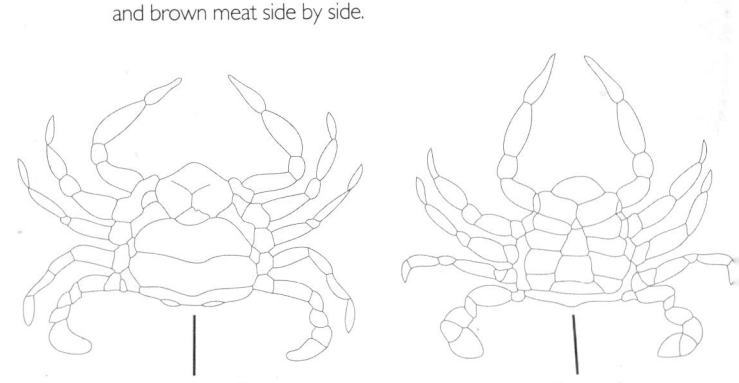

female crab   *male crab*